ISLINGTON

 KU-288-624

Please return this item on or before the last date stamped below or you may be liable to overdue charges. To renew an item call the number below, or access the online catalogue at www.islington.gov.uk/libraries. You will need your library membership number and PIN number.

2 20		
- 4 MAR 2020		

Islington Libraries

020 7527 6900   **www.islington.gov.uk/libraries**

ISLINGTON LIBRARIES

3 0120 02804192 9

RAISING
AN
EYEBROW
MY LIFE WITH
SIR ROGER MOORE

GARETH OWEN

The
History
Press

First published 2020

The History Press
97 St George's Place, Cheltenham,
Gloucestershire, GL50 3QB
www.thehistorypress.co.uk

© Gareth Owen, 2020

The right of Gareth Owen to be identified as the Author
of this work has been asserted in accordance with the
Copyright, Designs and Patents Act 1988.

All rights reserved. No part of this book may be reprinted
or reproduced or utilised in any form or by any electronic,
mechanical or other means, now known or hereafter invented,
including photocopying and recording, or in any information
storage or retrieval system, without the permission in writing
from the Publishers.

British Library Cataloguing in Publication Data.
A catalogue record for this book is available from the British Library.

ISBN 978 0 7509 9327 2

Typesetting and origination by The History Press
Printed and bound in Great Britain by TJ International Ltd.

MIX
Paper from
responsible sources
FSC® C013056
FSC
www.fsc.org

Contents

FOREWORD BY BRITT EKLAND

Having known Roger for many years as a friend and as a co-star in *The Man with the Golden Gun*, I can honestly say he was one of the most charming men I've ever met. He was also one of the busiest. He never stopped working: TV, film, writing books, touring his show and, of course, his work with UNICEF.

But when you are working that hard, there's always someone in the wings making sure it's all running smoothly. In Roger's case it was his long-time private secretary, Gareth Owen.

Gareth knew Roger better than anyone, even some of his wives, and he could usually second-guess and keep one step ahead of him, which was invaluable.

But beyond that, they were the best of friends – that was so evident to anyone who saw them together. They were so very loyal to each other, and even shared the same naughty sense of humour …

I'm delighted Gareth has written about their years together. This book is insightful, fun, poignant and, just like their working relationship, so unique. Roger was indeed the nicest man ever!

PROLOGUE

The last time I saw Roger in person was early March 2016, a couple of months before he died.

I was leaving his chalet in Crans-Montana, Switzerland, after spending a week with him and his wife, Kristina, following his discharge from hospital in Lausanne to 'build up his strength' in readiness for his next round of cancer treatment. Whilst a tiny part of me knew it might be the last time I saw him, I never really thought it possible that my hero would ever die; he'd always said, when people asked him how he would like to be remembered, 'as the oldest person in the world' – and I believed him.

I prepared some of the leftover cottage pie I'd made him earlier in the week and left it in the microwave for Kristina to heat up along with some vegetables for his lunch, an hour or so later. He thanked me for coming and wished me a safe journey home, and Kristina hugged me tightly but silently – her silence spoke volumes. We were both still in shock that this was happening.

I got into the taxi that had pulled up outside – much to Roger's chagrin as he had wanted to drive me to the funicular station, despite being barely able to walk around his house – and waved goodbye. The five-minute drive to the station was so very full of emotion with various thoughts and worries running around my head. But it had been a good week – we'd worked on his book, we'd watched a few movies, I'd made him his favourite meals and we'd even ventured out to lunch once – so I convinced myself to be full of hope and optimism. The thirty-minute funicular trip, followed by a two-hour rail journey to Geneva airport and a flight back to Heathrow, was always a tiring adventure, more so this time as I couldn't stop thinking of him.

Roger and I spoke regularly in the days and weeks afterwards, and up until 12 April we saw each other on Skype video calls. That was the day of our last Skype call and after that the phone calls became more sporadic as his illness took a firmer grip on his mortality. The last time we actually spoke was a few days before he died, when his daughter Deborah was with him in hospital, in Sion, and she'd called me to say he wanted a word. I know he'd been drifting in and out of consciousness and when he greeted me with, 'Hello boyo, how are you?' in a very weak voice, I tried to think of something to reply; I couldn't say, 'Oh I'm fine, how are you?' because I knew exactly how he was, so instead said, 'It's so good to hear your voice.' Just then he gave out a moan of pain, and Deborah took the phone back to tell me he was trying to get comfortable in bed and she was going to adjust his pillows.

By the following week, he'd gone.

I'd never known a world without Roger Moore. Life suddenly seemed very strange, and eerily quiet.

CHAPTER 1

IMPRESSIONISTIC DAYS

Roger Moore is all around me – there are snaps and some posters on my office walls – and every day there is something to remind me of him, be it a conversation, a place, an experience, a film or TV show on the box, or just a happy thought. In fact, all my thoughts of Roger are happy, well, all but the last weeks of his life.

I miss him hugely because he was a *huge* part of my life, first as an actor and cinematic hero, then as my boss, my co-author, co-host and above all, my best friend, and I know I was one of his most trusted friends too. The relationship between any personal assistant and their boss is a close one, professionally speaking, and with Roger – although he was largely based overseas and I at his Pinewood office which he'd had since 1970 – we spoke regularly and spent time with one another in the office, at his home and in all corners of the world. A PA is a bit like a family member in that you are so much a part of their private life, their routines, their diary, their family, their woes and worries, their frustrations. Sometimes you're closer than family, and certainly always trusted as a member of the family.

I'm often asked, 'How did I come to work with him?' I quite often reply, 'There was a notice in the post office window saying, "Megastar needs new PA".'

'Really?' they ask, with great interest.

'No! Not quite,' I reply and evade giving a proper answer.

I suppose part of a PA's role is to be discreet, not to give anything away, and to be honest I'm a very private sort of person anyway; and I liken such questioning to a total stranger approaching you and saying, 'I hear you work at the bank, how did you get that gig?' or 'I hear you're a plumber, who gave you that job?' – that probably rarely happens I realise, but mention you work for someone famous and all of a sudden everyone's very interested. Curiosity? A hint of the untouchable?

But how *did* I get the job? Well, it's a long story involving a bit of a journey, which taught me a lot of skills, made me a lot of contacts and helped me develop as the person I am – all invaluable for ending up as a PA to an international megastar (tongue firmly placed in cheek).

I was born in 1973, the same year Roger Moore debuted as James Bond 007 in *Live and Let Die*. There must have been some serendipity, as he was to become my favourite film star and the James Bond series became something of an obsession with me – and he was of course was my favourite 007.

My parents were great cinema-goers, or as they would say, they liked 'going to the pictures'. I have several hazy memories of the Odeon in Chester, and my pushchair being left in the manager's office downstairs as I was carried up to the main screen upstairs, as there wasn't a lift. That was back in the days of having to queue to see a film, and the queues quite often stretched around the block into Northgate Street and the manager would walk down, counting people, and when he reached a point in the queue he'd apologise and say, 'the house is full beyond here'. I recall wanting to see *The Rescuers* (1977) and being turned away, only for my mum to persuade the manager to let her sit on one of the small fold-down usher seats at the back of the auditorium with me on her lap.

It was there at the Odeon, aged 4, that I saw *The Spy Who Loved Me* (1977). There was something magical about it, not least the white underwater Lotus Esprit car – a toy Corgi model of which I bashed and bruised with gusto during my own pretend adventures at home – and the villainous steel-toothed Jaws left a lasting impression. Though I loved going to the cinema – and had done so since being a babe in arms, my mother professes – there was something different about this trip, and the seeds were very much sown.

I had to wait until Christmas 1978 for my next taste of 007, four or five years before VHS and rental video shops appeared in the UK, when a Bond film premiered on television. It was the first time ITV had screened one of the series at Christmas, thus beginning a long tradition; however, I was shocked and horrified to discover it wasn't the real James Bond. It was someone else pretending to be 007! The film was *Diamonds Are Forever* (1971) and its star was a chap named Sean Connery. Despite protestations from within the house that he was the original James Bond, I couldn't nor wouldn't have it – I wanted Roger Moore.

The summer of 1979 came around, as did *Moonraker*, and I became more aware of the series and Roger's predecessors in the roles, though couldn't get my head around why George Lazenby made one and then Sean Connery came back – but then again, I'd challenge any 6-year-old to grasp the contractual ins and outs of life at United Artists (the films' distributor and financier). Though criticised for being more fantastical than believable, for a youngster who'd just lapped up *Star Wars* and *Close Encounters*, it was bang on the money of the space fascination adventures we were all enjoying.

I totally 'got' that Roger Moore was an actor and not just James Bond, and became aware of other films he'd made – though I hadn't been allowed to see the more violent ones such as *The Wild Geese*

(1978) – and there was also something about a TV series or two he'd done, but I had to wait a bit longer for those to come my way as the three TV channels we had weren't running them as, I was told, Roger Moore didn't want them on TV again. Actually, it was more to do with a royalties negotiation but as I say, you can't expect a 6-year-old to know much about all that. The more I saw of Moore on screen, the more I liked him; I liked him in interviews too, as he had a childish sense of fun and never took things too seriously. He soon became my favourite movie star and I'd cut pieces out of the newspaper and film brochures from the cinema lobby and yearned to see yet another new Bond film. Fortunately they were produced fairly regularly back then, coming out every two years.

I remember once watching the (then) popular *Fix It* programme on a Saturday early evening, where people wrote in to the show asking for the host to 'fix it for me to …' This particular episode featured Desmond Llewelyn who played Q in the Bond movies, and some young chap who wanted to meet him and get to look at the gadgets he made for 007. Desmond – a fellow Welshman – came across as being absolutely lovely, kind, generous and witty. He carried a battered old attaché case around with him that was featured in *From Russia With Love* (1963) where Q armed that other fellow with a few gadgets. None of them really worked; they were film props, but it was fascinating to hear Desmond talk about working on the films and laughing off his own technical 'uselessness'. So I thought I'd try my luck and write in to the programme, asking them to fix it for me to meet my hero, Roger Moore. I said it was my lifelong ambition – all eight or ten years of it – and took my carefully written and spelling-corrected letter to the post office, bought a first-class stamp and popped it in the post box.

I checked the mail delivery at home every day for weeks (months!) to see if any reply had come for me – we didn't have a telephone at home so it was the only contact I anticipated – and sure enough … nothing. Not a word, not an acknowledgement, nothing. 'Perhaps Roger is busy,' I told myself. I never gave up hope of one day meeting him.

I collected the odd bit of Bond memorabilia whenever I saw it – toy cars, a music LP, books, etc. – and eagerly awaited news of any new film, although the only way of garnering any titbits was through the odd story in a newspaper. Google hadn't been heard of, nor had the internet come to that. I'd drool over any behind-the-scenes photo that appeared in the *News of the World* 'from the set of the latest Bond film' – it was like manna from heaven.

I vividly remember going to see *Octopussy* (1983) when I was 10. We'd planned a summer camping trip to Prestatyn, near Rhyl in North Wales, with the four-man tent I'd had for Christmas the previous year. Life under canvas was to be a huge and new adventure, and once experienced, rarely sought after again. But a holiday without electricity or a television, even for a few days, proved a challenge when it came to the evenings; after a day out doing whatever we did, we returned to base for a camp meal and then wondered what to do. We could have talked, I suppose? No! We opted to 'go to the pictures' and it just so happened Rhyl had two cinemas at that time: the three-screen Apollo (a former Odeon) and the Plaza, a slightly less loved two-screen cinema that was soon to be closed and converted to an indoor market. The Apollo had the latest James Bond film, whilst the Plaza was screening *Star Wars: Return of the Jedi* (1983), so we got to see them both. *Octopussy* pitted the Russians against the good guys, offered an exciting chase on tuk-tuks, villains on elephants and even a hot air balloon coming to the rescue, plus the usual mix of gadgets, girls and Roger's own unique take on the character. There had been newspaper headlines about the 'Battle of the Bonds' as Sean Connery had been lured back to play Bond in the unofficial *Never Say Never Again* (1983), but the latter film had been pushed back to a Christmas release to avoid a head-to-head box office battle with the official series – though Roger of course played in the most successful of the two movies. Take that, Sean Connery!

I recall talk of Roger retiring after *Octopussy* as the critics were saying he was getting too long in the tooth to play 007 again. In fact, Roger later told me he had wanted to bow out and felt it was the perfect film to end on, as he'd really enjoyed making it and it had performed admirably at the box office. Financial temptation can be a wicked thing, though, and producer Cubby Broccoli teased him to the point of not being able to refuse returning in *A View to a Kill* (1985) – which I went to see at my beloved Chester Odeon, screen one, upstairs.

I was greatly saddened to hear Roger announce he was stepping down in 1986, after seven outings for Eon Productions, yet unlike his predecessors (and successors) he remained a wonderful ambassador for the franchise, always talking positively, embracing interviews and being fully supportive of the other actors who picked up the Walther PPK. But that was Roger all over; why be negative when you can be positive and be part of something popular? The desire to be loved was always his weakness.

Soon afterwards Roger hosted an ITV documentary celebrating *25 Years of James Bond* from what I thought was his own Swiss chalet – it was actually a location they'd hired. Roger never allowed film crews or journalists into his home (though *Hello* magazine did pay hugely for the privilege once or twice!) as he reasoned, for one thing, it was his personal, private space and he didn't want anyone commenting on or judging his taste, or worse, gossiping about it in print or on TV; and secondly, he reasoned that if he had based his company at home then he could have claimed a tax relief and that would have then been fair game to host interviews as it was a place of work, but actors never received such a tax break, so why should he allow his home to become a place of work in that sense? So he'd always request interviews be at a hotel or another venue, such as the local golf club – not that he played, he just dined there!

Timothy Dalton succeeded him as Bond, though Roger tactfully dodged any questions about what he thought of Dalton in the part by simply smiling and saying, 'I've never seen his films I'm afraid.'

It was around this time that I became aware I wasn't alone as a Bond fan. Up until then it had seemed as though, as popular as the films were, they hadn't the visible fan base that *Star Wars, Back to the Future, Indiana Jones*, etc. had, where their memorabilia was everywhere and it was cool to say they were your favourite movies. Bond seemed to be a bit more underground, but that changed when I discovered the James Bond Fan Club.

In 1990 it was announced the fan club would be holding a convention – its first in a few years – at Pinewood Studios, the home of the James Bond movies. Wow. What's more, via an advert in the *007 Magazine* I'd learned about a 007 Collectors' Club run by the lovely Dave Worrall, and through that club my own little Bond collection started swelling with purchases of posters, books, toys, merchandise – one item being a '50 Years of Pinewood Studios' publication from 1986, with some terrific features including a chapter on 007, and furthermore it mentioned that Roger Moore still had an office at the studio. The chance of visiting the Bond Mecca that is Pinewood, along with maybe walking past his office, was a temptation too great to resist, so off I went to the building society to cash in some savings and send a cheque for £100 to the fan club for a one-day ticket (the two-day ticket plus extra accommodation was a little out of my savings' grasp I'm afraid). Happily I was one of the successful 200 attendees, and on 29 September 1990 walked through the gates of Pinewood – home of Bond, *Carry On*, Norman Wisdom, *Superman* and so many other great films – for the very first time.

It was a day that changed my life.

CHAPTER 2

PINEWOOD BO(U)ND

Following the convention's morning film screening of *From Russia with Love* (1963), we fans were escorted to the Pinewood canteen for lunch. There were a few journalists in attendance and one ambled over to me and asked if he could have a word, introducing himself as being from one of the local area newspapers. I dare say some journalists were there to do a fun piece on 200 geeky fans turning up in anoraks and clutching plastic carrier bags full of tat, but this chap seemed genuinely enthusiastic about being there himself. He asked the inevitable, 'Who is your favourite James Bond actor?'

'Roger Moore,' I said proudly.

I should point out that by this point Timothy Dalton had made two films and was widely praised as being 'the best ever James Bond', but as I've gone through life I've generally found the present incumbent is usually hailed as the best, though Sean Connery – being the first and original – still holds a huge affection and respect amongst fans.

'And why Roger Moore?' my interviewer asked with genuine interest; perhaps he'd never met a live RM fan before?

'Because I identify with his sense of humour,' was my considered reply.

'Good answer!' he said, before going off in search of the George Lazenby fan.

It was then that Dave Worrall, from the Collectors' Club, stepped forward as our tour host – he was going to take us on a walk around the studio.

Nondescript corridors became places of marvel as we looked at the film posters adorning the walls, and then when we all turned a corner the huge '007 Stage' stood in front of us, dominating the landscape, and what's more we had permission to go on there. In walking around Pinewood it became apparent this was a once much-loved studio now down on its luck with peeling paintwork, crumbling walls, workshops propped and patched up; it was exciting yet sad to see. Adjacent to the 007 Stage was a gated set; security men were there to open up and allow us to venture on – it was the Gotham City set from Tim Burton's *Batman* (1989) which had been left standing for the proposed sequel, which alas never materialised – at Pinewood. We walked around, ran up the steps of City Hall and snapped away with cameras. As though that wasn't excitement enough, we were then escorted to B-Stage where the large soundproof door was raised to reveal an Aladdin's cave of Bond treasures – Aston Martin and Lotus cars, props, costumes, models and a number of actors including Desmond Llewelyn, seated behind tables in readiness to sign autographs (for free!). When I eventually worked my way around to Desmond, he asked my name and then asked if I was Welsh.

'Yes, from Wrexham,' I replied.

That seemed to delight him as he was once stationed in the town with the Royal Welsh Guards and he chatted away to me for ages – well, probably a minute or two – but I was so touched and so delighted.

I left Pinewood that night with a spring in my step. Not only had I met 200 fellow Bond fans, I'd spent the most magical day at the most famous film studio in the world. Aged 17 and studying A levels, I hadn't really decided what I wanted to do for a career and had toyed with 'safe' jobs such as banking or teaching, but that day at Pinewood changed all that. I was determined I wanted to work in the film industry, and not just anywhere – I wanted to work at Pinewood, to have my own office and parking space there and maybe, one day, just happen to bump into Roger Moore.

As luck would have it, I was able to return to Pinewood in spring 1991 when Dave Worrall launched his book *The Most Famous Car in the World* there, which was all about the Aston Martin DB5 as made famous by Sean Connery driving it in *Goldfinger* (1964) and *Thunderball* (1965). Dave had been trying to get the book published for some time, but the traditional, big publishers all told him it was too niche and too specialised to stand any chance of being commercial. Long before self-publishing was economical, Dave decided to go out on a limb and publish the book himself and figured if he had several hundred subscribers to his magazine, chances were he could pre-sell a quantity, which would in turn help offset the upfront costs. That's exactly what he did and turned out a terrifically well-researched, -written and -designed tome – that sells for hundreds of pounds nowadays. Anyhow, his launch party was at Pinewood and featured a number of Bond alumni and gave me a chance to reacquaint myself with the studio once more.

Bond conventions at Pinewood actually became annual events from 1992 onwards for four or five years, always lavishly put together by Graham Rye, with various guests from the series ranging from George Lazenby to Lois Maxwell (Miss Moneypenny), Christopher Lee (Scaramanga), Desmond Llewelyn (Q), Maurice Binder (titles designer), Peter Lamont (production designer), Guy Hamilton (director) and others. Though he was always invited, Roger Moore never attended – I was thwarted again!

I'd meanwhile drifted into university in 1991 – I say drifted because I had no firm career plan, other than aspirations, and if nothing else it was one way of buying me time to decide what I might go on to do and how I might achieve it. I arrived at Bangor University, it being the most appealing of the ones I visited because it was in a relatively small city, on the seaside in beautiful North Wales and it had a decent reputation. My first year accommodation was in halls and I made some good friends both there and on my Electronic Engineering course, which, after the first foundation year, I switched to Applied Physics and Electronics; the main difference being there was more physics than there was computer engineering, as whilst I didn't (and don't) mind using computers I have no desire to get to know how to design and program them.

I had a bit of a bee in my bonnet at the time about the film industry, which really was in the doldrums, and I remember reading in the early 1990s that there were on average fifteen British films produced a year; it was no wonder Pinewood looked a bit tired and unloved last time I visited. It was as though I had an uncanny knack of opening a newspaper or magazine, or switching on the TV or radio, where there'd be someone bemoaning the state of British film, the lack of support the industry received – in comparison to the French and Irish industries – and the mass exodus of our talent overseas. Richard Attenborough and David Puttnam were usually brought in to comment and I think there was a feeling of, 'Oh no, not them again.' Yes, they were successful Oscar winners who cared passionately for the business, but I felt they were becoming overused – public empathy is a strange thing, and when rich, successful film-makers bemoan they can't get films made it didn't really rouse people into action.

Whilst realising a 19-year-old physics student couldn't do much to help, I thought I should at least be more aware of the problems and obstacles facing British film-makers and what better way than to contact some of them? I first wrote to my MP (Labour) to see what government support there was (or wasn't?) particularly after reading of the huge importance the French government placed on their industry: a flag-carrying, culturally crucial part of French life. I was of course told of the bold plans with which Labour hoped to develop to support the industry, should they get into power at the next election, and the lack of the current Tory administration's support for it – free enterprise should, the Tory party believed, sink or swim on its own merits. It wasn't a government's role to prop it up.

I wrote to the Tory administration: there wasn't a film minister or Department of Culture back then; film fell under the remit of the minister of trade, further underlining the government's lack of interest in fostering a native film business. I received a rather condescending letter back telling me the government fully supported British film, and as such were 'giving' £14 million annually to the British Film Institute and furthermore investing £5 million over three years as 'pump priming finance' in the Eurimages initiative of the EU. Yet back then the BFI was chiefly concerned with preserving film, supporting education, publishing and offering a modest production fund to a few select film-makers. It wasn't anything like the funding body of today and didn't play any role in government policy.

So why was the business languishing? Was there a lack of appetite for home-grown product? Was there a lack of cinema screens? Was there a lack of decent distribution? I think the answer to those and other questions was 'yes'. Peter Greenaway was making films, as were Ken Loach and Mike Leigh, but they were not particularly wide appealing, and were viewed as art house, whereas American imported films were cleaning up at the box office. Distributors such as Rank (which also owned Odeon) struck deals with American producers to supply their company with products in exchange for minimal investments (and risk) – and there were so many American films to choose from.

Feeling a little frustrated I sought views from veteran film-makers, actors, writers, distributors, presenters and just about as many other places as I could think of and one thing became clear – the UK was not a welcoming environment for film-makers. There was no logistical support to filming in big cities, there were no tax breaks or incentives.

A few years earlier Lewis Gilbert took his production of *Educating Rita* to Dublin; he was about to be followed by Mel Gibson with *Braveheart* when, after setting up in Scotland, Gibson found little support and help yet the Irish offered him their army to serve as extras and a tax incentive. The last Bond film, *Licence to Kill*, had decamped from its traditional home at Pinewood to Mexico for better tax deals too.

It struck me that – whilst I didn't understand all the tax implications – there was a benefit to having a big production move in, not least in employment and local spend, but also in attracting others to follow. Britain was at risk of losing out. Continuing my research into the problems and potential solutions, I knew I'd only make headway if I could garner some serious names in support. To my surprise, and delight, they came thick and fast: Anthony Hopkins, Jeremy Irons, Bob Hoskins, John Cleese, Emma Thompson, Julie Walters, Bryan Forbes, Michael Relph, Roy Boulting, Guy Hamilton ... and many others. It certainly helped me gain some headlines in trade magazines and this 19-year-old physics student suddenly became someone making a noise from the public's point of view. *Film Review* magazine ran a feature on me and asked 'what next?' Thinking on my feet I announced, 'a showcase of British film – a British film weekend to really hammer home what we have done and what we can do again.'

But where? When?

I went out on a limb and contacted the manager of Theatr Clwyd – a huge theatre, gallery and cinema complex in Mold, North Wales – and in my letter explained that I wanted to stage a weekend event. I didn't get a reply, so after about ten days I wrote again and said I'd follow up in a phone call, which is exactly what I did – and I think I caught him on the hop as he invited me over for a meeting, although I could sense the reluctance in his voice. Elis Jones turned out to be a very jolly, friendly guy who was actually titled 'Programme Manager' and in charge of looking after the venue's calendar. We had a chat where I said I'd like to put together eight films in a single weekend: a Bond, a *Carry On*, a

Hammer Horror, a modern classic, a classic classic … and so on. He liked the idea though questioned the costs involved in programming eight films, as the licences alone would be upwards of £100 per film regardless of whether anyone came to see them. I cavalierly said, 'leave that to me' and we agreed provisional dates for the end of February 1993.

I contacted some local companies for potential sponsorship – but none were interested. A sound recordist friend of mine suggested I think outside the box, and approach film companies instead – Kodak being one. To my great delight Kodak came back and said, 'We'd like to support you, call us.' I spoke to Managing Director Geoff Cadogan and he said he was thinking of writing a cheque for £500, but needed to know where it would be spent – the bar was not an option. I suggested he sponsored the cost of the print hire – he agreed. I also managed to persuade one of the distributors to let us have their film for free, so I'd like to think Elis Jones was pleased his punt on me wasn't going to cost him – well, not much.

The next step was to round up physical support and invite celebrity guests. Of course, getting them to travel to North Wales and stay over was another expense, but one Elis said he'd happily help cover as they had a friendly local hotel. Sadly, and as enthusiastic as he'd been to attend, Anthony Hopkins wrote to say his filming schedule on a BBC movie in South Wales would prevent him, but he said he'd be up at Theatr Clwyd soon to discuss a production and invited me to join him and his wife for lunch nearby. He was lovely, and we chatted for an hour or more about everything and he said he could see my passion and enthusiasm and wanted to support that. He offered to pay for lunch, but even though I could barely afford it I insisted I should pay and gritted my teeth as I opened the bill. It was about £60 – but for a student in the early 1990s, that was a couple of weeks' food money!

For the weekend itself, I was fortunate my (now) friend Desmond Llewelyn said he'd come to represent the Bonds; Jack Douglas, the *Carry Ons*; and husband and wife Timothy West and Prunella Scales (who starred with Anthony Hopkins in one of the screened films, *A Chorus of Disapproval*) came too.

It was a really great weekend, with lots of media coverage. I was also asked, 'So what next?'

'We'll do it all again but this time in the south. At Pinewood Studios!' I exclaimed.

I'd previously interviewed the new managing director of the studio, Steve Jaggs, in my 'what's wrong and how might we overcome it' research – which I was about to publish and submit to the newly formed Department of Culture along with a petition of thousands of names I'd collected at local cinemas during my university holidays, requesting the government take seriously the need for the industry to receive some support. I suggested a tax break similar to the Irish, a small levy on video cassettes (the rapidly growing home media market) and the establishment of a British Film Week in cinemas on an annual basis.

The Department of Culture were aware I was travelling down to present my report and petition, and I think had an office junior on standby to meet and thank me at noon – high noon. But things took an exciting twist when the afternoon prior, having arrived in London, the ITV local news contacted me saying they wanted to be with me on the day – having seen reports on the ITV Wales local news a few days prior – and what's more, they arranged for Michael Winner to meet me ahead of going into the department. The instructions from Winner were very specific, to meet him at his house at 10.30 a.m. in Kensington and then we could go on to Westminster.

I arrived a few minutes early, and the TV crew a minute or so after me – the reporter was Rachel Friend, ex-*Neighbours* star, which was quite surreal given I used to watch the lunchtime edition every day during my uni lunch break.

Winner was charming, very kind and hugely complimentary towards me – though told the crew exactly where to set up, how to light it and how long they'd got! From there we crossed London to Trafalgar Square where the department said I was welcome, but could not go inside with a camera. Who cares, I was getting the support of Michael Winner and a TV news crew was in tow.

I was obviously being taken seriously and my merry band of 'celebrity supporters' was growing.

Steve Jaggs, at Pinewood, was gracious enough to invite me down for a chat, though I knew he had huge reservations about allowing me to take over the studio for a day of film screenings and celebrations. The last time they'd opened the gates to the public (outside of the Bond conventions) was in 1976 for the studio's fortieth anniversary – they'd expected a few hundred and a few thousand descended, blocking roads for miles around, and the local council said 'never again'. Of course, the studio was also a working facility and wouldn't want any of its customers annoyed by members of the public traipsing around.

I explained to Steve that I envisioned limiting the day to 150-200 attendees, screening three films, holding a lunch, gala dinner and having celebrity guests and displays throughout the day.

He was actually very receptive.

We agreed on a date in fact, 9 April 1994, and it was to be entitled British Film Day at Pinewood.

The day soon came around and with a terrific line-up of film vehicles outside to greet attendees, thanks to my old friend Robin Harbour tracking them down, and actors from Pinewood films including Sylvia Syms, Burt Kwouk, Valerie Leon, Liz Fraser, Jack Douglas, Bryan Forbes, Nannette Newman, Walter Gotell, Eunice Gayson and many others came to join us. Walter came with his wife, Celeste, one of the editors from the *Daily Express*, and she chatted to me about the day, my aspirations and just how old I was. She couldn't believe it when I said I was 20 and just about to start my final year exams. Walter sat me down and told me he had a script he was producing as a feature and that we should chat.

Again, I was fortunate to receive some good media coverage, including a couple of pages in *Empire* magazine which, amongst several other letters, prompted a missive from a businessman named Zygi Kamasa. He wrote that he owned a computer company in Uxbridge and was also a huge film fan, and had toyed with the idea of moving into the film industry but didn't have any clue as to how to go about it, and whilst he had money behind him he didn't have any contacts. He seemed to think I might be able to help him.

His offices were a few miles from Pinewood, so I suggested on my next trip down (with Robin Harbour) we should meet. Well, any excuse to visit the studio and catch up with some of my new friends who helped make British Film Day so enjoyable – including a thank you to Doris Spriggs, Roger Moore's PA who arranged for some signed memorabilia for our charity raffle.

I explained to Zygi that I'd teamed up with a friend in North Wales to set up a production company and after my exams and graduation would be looking to get some projects off the ground. Such was the British film industry that the only 'way in' for people like me was as a runner or to jump in at the deep end doing your own thing. I'd have loved to have been a runner but with fifteen films being made, there weren't exactly loads of opportunities … so it was the deep end for me!

Zygi asked what I knew about the business. I said, 'What *don't* I know?!'

Oh the arrogance of youth!

I went out on a limb and suggested to Zygi that if he wanted to go into a loose partnership, the ideal would be to take an office at Pinewood and set up shop. He liked the idea and suggested he'd be willing to pay the running costs, if I helped him with introductions and manned the office; all I'd need to do is cover my living expenses after graduation.

And that is the slightly abridged story of how I came to open an office at Pinewood, aged 21.

CHAPTER 3

WOULD YOU RELIEVE ME?

Having raised a few thousand pounds from well-meaning friends, I had a very tight but workable budget to relocate and base out of Pinewood. I mentioned my plans to Walter Gotell and he invited me to dinner the next time I was in London – well, there was lots to organise and I knew I would be down at least once or twice ahead of the 14 August relocation date.

Walter's apartment was in a very wealthy street in Westminster. Located on the second floor, it was probably four times the size of my mum's house in Wales, with a huge sitting room, dining room, three bedrooms, two bathrooms and kitchen.

Walter cooked a chicken meal, and rather than dish up the potatoes and vegetables he placed the saucepans on the table and grinned, 'It'll save on the washing up.'

Of course, I loved hearing tales from his career, his time on the Bond films as Russian General Gogol and working with the likes of Humphrey Bogart in *The African Queen*. Walter had a story for every occasion.

He then passed me a copy of a script he'd written, *The Knot*, which he explained was an Ireland-set story that had almost been made a few years earlier, but at the last minute the financing fell through. Although full of enthusiasm for it, I felt Walter's energy had been depleted and the thought of trying to mount it again himself proved daunting. 'It has Martin Sheen attached,' he told me, 'and Kevin Connor to direct.'

Over dinner he asked where I'd be living when I moved down to Pinewood. I said I hadn't really thought about it, and was just going to book into the local B&B and have a look around for somewhere.

'There's a room here,' he replied.

He took me down the hallway to a large double room.

'Our guest room. We've had lodgers before. Would you be interested? If so I'll check with Celeste.'

Picking up on the word 'lodgers' I realised it wasn't a freebie offer but Walter didn't mention money, so neither did I. I thanked him and said I needed to work a few things out and would be in touch, and that I also looked forward to reading his script.

The Knot was an IRA thriller. There had been so many films and TV programmes about the troubles in Northern Ireland that I immediately felt I'd heard it all before. Although I hadn't read that many scripts in my time, I liked to think I'd seen enough films to know what was good and what constituted a decent story. Alas *The Knot* was neither. I suggested to a friend that the only way it would go anywhere was if I gave it to a passing tramp – but Walter had been kind to me and I felt I should try and help him.

I thought about his offer of lodgings and whilst it would involve an hour commute each way to Pinewood every morning and evening, I liked the idea of being central, being in a nice apartment and with Walter – he was good fun and knew lots of people. I called him up and asked if his offer still stood. 'Yes, shall we say £50 a week?' he asked.

I had recently been paying about £35 rent a week at university, so in that context it was a bit more than I'd been used to, but of course this was central London!

The office at Pinewood was in the very centre of the studio, and Zygi came in once a week or so, which left me pretty much on my own – though looking at the four walls realising I had six months to get something under way was a huge spur to creativity.

I suggested to Walter it might be a good idea if I could speak with Kevin Connor about the script. He immediately went on the defensive, treating my request with suspicion. I reassured him it was only really to say hello and chat about his availability, which seemed to appease Walter although he was reluctant to give me Kevin's phone number, mumbling something about him being away filming. As coincidence would have it, a couple of days later BBC Radio 2's afternoon programme featured the host Gloria Hunniford visiting a film set in Dublin's Ardmore Studios, where they were filming *Great Expectations* with Peter Ustinov – the director just so happened to be Kevin Connor.

I rang Ardmore and eventually got through to the Irish co-producer of that film, Morgan O'Sullivan, who explained that Kevin was back in LA editing, but gave me the phone number of the cutting room. I called and asked if Kevin was available – he was. He greeted me warmly, but then hesitated. 'What do you think of the script?' he asked.

'To be honest,' I replied, 'I have some doubts.'

Kevin sighed with relief. He explained that he'd met Walter at a party in LA at Barbara Broccoli's house and Walter had pitched him the story, saying he had Martin Sheen attached. Of course, Kevin was very receptive to the idea … and then read the script.

'You know how it is,' he explained. 'I like Walter as a mate and only really agreed to do it because I never really thought he'd get it off the ground – and now you come along saying you're trying to get it going, which is great, but I'm worried about that script. There's a good idea in there, but it needs work.'

We continued chatting and Kevin suggested I speak with a writer friend of his, who might have a few thoughts and ideas. I liked Kevin.

My next approach was to Martin Sheen's agent. He just so happened to be Walter's agent too and told me – because Walter was a mate, etc. – Martin agreed to do it, but never expected it to actually get off the ground.

I was learning fast about the politics, or rather the bullshit, of showbusiness.

I think Walter was oblivious to his script needing work, and in fact told me he wouldn't change any of it – even when the IRA ceasefire was declared. 'We'll just put in a line about it being a phony ceasefire,' he exclaimed.

I liked Walter but found his intransigence very frustrating, but he wasn't the sort of character you could have a constructive conversation with – he'd just thrust a glass of Scotch into my hand (I hated Scotch) and tell me again how perfect the script was.

Pitching a script to potential financiers and distributors whilst knowing it needed work wasn't a recipe for success.

On a social level, Walter and Celeste were charming hosts. I pretty much kept myself to myself so as not to get in their way, and ate at the studio every lunchtime and in the evenings just grabbed a sandwich or went out to the cinema and had a snack there. On returning, I'd often find the apartment full of food as Celeste was the food column editor for her newspaper – one week she'd be trying out apple pie, the next it might be sausages, or burgers, or cheese. She'd have samples from all the major supermarkets and stores ranging from Waitrose to the Co-op, M&S, Tesco, Asda, Sainsbury's and so on. Celeste quite often gave me parcels to distribute to my neighbours at the studio; though if it was ever alcohol she was sampling, Walter ensured none of it strayed far from him.

One particularly evening I arrived back about 11.00 p.m. after a film and crept in quietly so as not to disturb them. Within a minute I could hear Walter shuffling down the corridor, with his heavy, slow breathing.

'Good evening?' he asked.

'Yes, I've been to the cinema …'

He sat down on the blanket box at the end of my bed, in his crisp white nightshirt, crossing his bare legs.

'Who was in it?' he asked in his deep, drawn-out, sotto voice.

After my short critique, Walter looked at me and said, 'Listen. I wonder … [breath] … would you do me a favour … [breath] … and relieve me … [he shuffled on his seat and uncrossed his legs, breath] …'

My blood ran cold for what seemed like a couple of minutes, and my face must have looked a picture of horror.

'… of some pavlova?' he concluded his sentence.

It seemed Celeste was tasting the meringue dessert and there was lots left over that wouldn't fit in the fridge.

I laughed in joyous relief. 'Of course, Walter, I'll do my best.'

He told me he had received an offer of a guest role in *The X-Files* and would be flying out to LA the following week. 'They're buying me flexible business flights with Virgin,' he added, 'and I'll cash them in and just book economy. That'll be my spending money for a couple of weeks. Will you be okay to keep an eye on Celeste?'

I think his trip to LA was really the beginning of the end of the film project and our working relationship. He was aware that Martin Sheen was being less than enthusiastic about the movie, and from LA phoned me to say he had bumped into his old friend Pierce Brosnan.

'He's Irish and needs a good film,' he told me.

'But Walter, he's just been signed as the new Bond!'

'Yes, yes, yes. I know, but he'll need a good dramatic piece to follow up with,' he reasoned.

'Has he read the script?' I asked.

'Doesn't need to. He'll do it for me.'

'Walter, he really needs to read the script. It does need some work.'

'Nonsense!' he said and ended the conversation.

I reported back to Kevin Connor, who said he'd heard from Walter and was going to have a coffee with him and express some reservations.

Walter's next phone call to me came a few days later.

'Forget Pierce,' he said, 'I've got a much better idea.'

'Who?'

'Burt Reynolds!' he exclaimed with pride.

'Burt Reynolds? When did he last make a film?'

This was genuinely a period when Reynolds found it difficult to get arrested, let alone land a starring role in a film.

'I think Kevin …' I began.

'Never mind Kevin, I've other ideas for directors now.'

I sensed we were going nowhere fast.

On his return to London, Walter hadn't been terribly well and suffered a reoccurrence of stomach cancer, but said, 'Oh they'll just cut it out and I'll be fine.'

I went to visit him at the London Clinic, off Harley Street, soon after he'd had his surgery, and he seemed upbeat and optimistic. I told him I'd spoken with the agent Mike Ovitz in LA and he'd said Jeff Bridges was available and interested – but added quickly – based on the changes Kevin wants made to the script.

He mumbled something about Jeff Bridges not having the edge of Burt Reynolds – I put that down to his pain medication! – but smiled and said we'd talk more on his return home. Actually, a few days after heading back to the apartment, Walter said he and Celeste were going off to Ireland to his 'castle' – as he called it – and had written the turreted house into his script, saying he expected a facility fee if we filmed there.

I was quite relieved to see him leave and had some serious conversations with Kevin about the impasse we'd reached – we had a script, written by a man who knew deep down it needed work, yet wouldn't admit it and anyone who questioned him was dismissed. Even Jeff Bridges – subject to script changes – didn't convince him.

I couldn't go on; I felt terribly torn. I was loyal to Walter and appreciated his friendship, but the clock was ticking and it was costing me money – I needed to make progress on a project to try and secure some more vitally important running and living costs. I'd spent almost a year working on *The Knot*, and I'd also acquired a couple of other scripts which I felt stood a better chance of moving forward. Walter was still away, and knowing how difficult it would be trying to speak with him – as he'd summarily dismiss any of my doubts – I wrote to him. I explained as the option he'd granted me on his script was about to run out, and as there was no feasible progress, then I had no alternative but to say thank you, move on and move out.

I returned to the apartment, packed up my things and left a card thanking them both from the bottom of my heart, but saying I just couldn't continue. I walked out the front door and felt such a sense of relief – I really had been unhappy and so stressed, but only realised it at that moment.

Prior to moving into Pinewood I had been a judge at the Co-op Young People's Film Festival for a couple of years (thanks to an introduction by Robin Harbour), and as part of our judging we were ensconced for a weekend watching VHS copies of short films from young film-makers. I think for every entry the youngsters received £50, and for every entry selected to go forward they received £100, so a few canny young directors submitted three or four films to earn a few quid. We soon realised there was a young guy who submitted annually, and who made very good, fun, short films – and showed great promise. The following year he and a couple of others were invited along to meet us. Over a drink I chatted with him and he said his ambition was to make a full-length feature film before he turned 20, and he gave me a script entitled *A Fistful of Fingers* – a spaghetti western set in Somerset.

He asked if I could help him get it made. His name was Edgar Wright.

A few months later he told me he'd met a producer through the Raindance Festival who felt he could pull together a deal, based on finance Edgar had raised from some sponsors, but he still needed help. Ultimately I introduced him to Zygi Kamasa who agreed to plug the financing gap, and having shot the movie in a month, Edgar was delighted that Pinewood had offered him a cutting room at the studio; he was going to stay with his brother in Ealing and as it was on my way in/out of London every day I offered to pick him up and drop him off occasionally to save him the train fare.

Edgar offered me an executive producer credit.

I used to see quite a bit of Edgar around the studio, and he was delighted when I introduced him to Norman Wisdom, who in turn I'd met at a charity lunch and who just so happened to have a long-cherished film script he wanted to get made. Norman became a good mate actually, though try as we did, over a couple of years we just couldn't close the finance to make his story, *Adam & Evil*, which is one of the few great sadnesses of my life.

I'd kept in touch with Anthony Hopkins in the intervening year or two, and told him I was working with Norman – in the hope he'd agree to making a little cameo. A few days later his PA Katherine phoned. 'Tony was wondering would it be possible for him to have lunch with Norman? He's going to be making the Picasso film at Pinewood soon, so maybe when Norman is in next?'

Norman seemed quite chuffed at the idea, though was slightly worried about 'will he ask to eat my liver with a nice Chianti?'

On the day in question I walked with Norman down to the dining room, where Tony Hopkins was already seated. He leapt up, smiled widely and hugged Norman.

A couple of hours later, Norman returned and said, 'That Tony is a nice bloke.'

Meanwhile, Edgar Wright's producer had formed an alliance with Zygi to produce a low-budget film, based on a Thomas Hardy novel – *The Scarlet Tunic*. When I say low-budget you must remember this is before digital film-making and inexpensive cameras made film-making on pocket-money budgets remotely viable; their budget was to be a couple of hundred thousand pounds. They raised the budget through advertising in the *Evening Standard* newspaper – invest £1,000 and be an extra. It was all done under a tax incentive called the Enterprise Investment Scheme, where 20 per cent of an investment could be offset against tax – handy for people with big bills looming – and profits would be tax free.

They shot the film, though struggled to get it released and so decided to self-distribute – literally selling into cinemas directly. I think they managed to get quite a few screens to show it for a day here and there, and with DVD sales managed to make their money back. Through it, Zygi realised the real money was made in distribution and not production, and after making another low-budget film, he formed a small distribution company and managed to get some financial backing. They released a few successful movies – including *Bend It Like Beckham* – under their banner and eventually were bought out by a major, Lionsgate. Zygi became managing director of Lionsgate UK under the deal where he still resides today, releasing hit after hit.

From someone who 'knew nothing' about the film industry he'd certainly learned quickly!

Edgar Wright hasn't done too badly for himself either. From his first film he went on to direct some TV, pop videos and then had a massive hit with a movie called *Shaun of the Dead* which has certainly led him to even greater success since.

CHAPTER 4

MOVE INTO WRITING (AND ROGER'S OFFICE)

The film business, and Pinewood in particular, was an exciting place to work though you could quite often spend months (if not years) working on a project – sending out scripts, budgets, sales forecasts, attending meetings, discussing finance – and get nowhere. Of course, the rent still had to be paid as did the photocopying and postage bill.

I was fortunate to secure some lottery money in the development of one of the scripts I'd optioned, which helped, but on a bit of a punt I contacted a trade magazine that was distributed around the studio every few months to ask if they were looking for any articles. I'm not quite sure why I thought I could be one of their writing team, but I guess you'll try anything when you're hungry? The answer came back, 'Yes, production-related articles and we pay 20p a word.' I immediately thought that a one-page, 500-word article would pay £100, so why not write a 2,000-word article and earn £400 – that was the rent for a month!

There were quite a few films shooting in and around London, and I literally selected one and phoned the publicist to ask if I could do an on-set feature. They willingly agreed and I found myself at a converted warehouse in Camberwell late one night – I chatted with the director, writer, producer and put together my article. The editor seemed to like it and suggested we meet for lunch. It wasn't so much a grand restaurant as the Red Cow pub in Richmond, opposite their offices, where he bought me a sandwich and drink, told me he wanted me to write more but with a 'slant towards advertisers'. I asked what that meant and he explained, 'Mention what cameras they're using, what film stock, who processes it, who supplies the lighting, the transport, the catering … and then we'll try and get those companies to advertise.'

I became quite adept at dropping in various names, suppliers, contractors and facilities into my articles and regularly supplied two or three features to each issue. I then had the idea of profiling some actors, and of course the first on my list was Roger Moore.

I'd got to know his PA at Pinewood, Doris Spriggs, on a 'Hello, how are you?' chat type basis. I dropped a copy of the published magazine in to her and she in turn dropped me a note a few days later saying she'd enjoyed it and 'well done'. I mentioned to her I was thinking of writing a book about Pinewood, as I'd been so fortunate to get to know so many wonderful characters around the studio, all with tales to tell and a book written through their eyes would really bring the story to life, I felt. Doris told me a few little interesting stories about some of the films she'd worked on as a production secretary; she'd actually been in Hollywood for a few years and worked on big films such as *The Sand Pebbles*, *The Quiet American*, *Tora! Tora! Tora!* and others before returning to the UK for family commitments, which is when she really did answer an ad on the Pinewood notice board for 'Wanted: secretary for Roger Moore.'

It was a Sunday in December 1999 when I caught a headline on the TV news saying, 'Bond actor dies in crash.'

My heart sank. There weren't many people who would warrant a news headline such as this from the series, and when I realised it was my friend Desmond Llewelyn I burst into tears. He really had become a great friend, and we met regularly for lunch either at Pinewood, at his home in Bexhill or halfway somewhere. I'd even stayed with him and his wife Pamela and he'd always been so supportive.

The next day I went to see Doris and she told me Roger had phoned her the evening before, having seen Sky News, and said he really sounded very upset, and hugely saddened.

A couple of weeks later I attended Desmond's funeral in Hastings. The church was packed and many of his Bond alumni attended, and although Roger was overseas working, he had firmly committed to attend Desmond's memorial service a few months later.

Meanwhile, my friend Brian Burford had written some articles for various magazines and I knew he wanted to take a step up, so I suggested to him that we might collaborate on my proposed Pinewood book. I would write the main text, but if he could handle some of the big chapters like *Carry On, Bond* and *Superman* that'd be great. For six or seven months I interviewed people, wrote to others and read as many books and trade journals about film production in the UK as I could. In the late 1990s, websites like IMDB weren't that comprehensive and many films were 'missing' cast lists, crew lists and any statistics, so I had to go about it the old-fashioned way with film guidebooks and trade magazines from the different periods. I interviewed over 100 people ranging from prop men to editors, producers, actors, directors, writers and production managers (Brian covered quite a few additional interviews too). Some of my subjects were fairly elderly, and in fact one of the first producers based at Pinewood, Anthony Havelock-Allan, was then 95 and in poor health, but his memory was razor sharp and he told me all about his early association with David Lean on films such as *Brief Encounter*, *Oliver Twist* and *Great Expectations*. I felt so fortunate to meet these great people, capturing their memories for future generations.

I asked Doris if Roger Moore might be part of the book, but she said his schedule was pretty hectic then. However, she said if I left her a few questions she'd get answers; she also said he might consider writing the foreword if I'd like. I didn't need to think about it – of course I'd like!

Maybe I'd impressed Doris, or maybe she realised I had a real passion for what I was doing, but from that point on we enjoyed regular chats, and she occasionally asked if I could look things up for her on the internet. She herself was a technophobe, only having a typewriter and fax machine in the office, so things that would have taken her a day to research I could miraculously conjure up in a few minutes. One day she phoned me in a bit of a flustered state. She said Mrs Moore (Luisa) had asked her to compile a list of private schools in the M25 area for a friend. 'I'll have to go to the library and get all the phone directories for the different areas out and shortlist them that way,' she said, 'but wondered do you have any ideas on the internet?'

Ten minutes later I knocked on her door and presented her with eight A4 pages of schools with contact details. Her face lit up. I'd obviously saved her a day in the library, but had also presented her with everything required swiftly. 'I can fax this right over,' she said, 'and then that's done!'

After *The Pinewood Story* was published, I wrote another book about one of the really fascinating characters I'd met during my research of that first book. Albert (Bert) Luxford was a special effects engineer, and along with making most of the gadgets in the early Bond films, worked on masses of other films adding 'little gimmicks' as he called them. Everything from blowing up things to making daggers, guns and even swords for the original *Highlander* film. He had a very dry sense of humour and knew how to tell a good tale – the book was a total joy to work on with Bert.

Desmond's memorial service came around. It was held at a church in Knightsbridge and afterwards we were all invited to an adjacent hotel for drinks – that was the first time I ever met Roger. He'd spoken at the memorial and afterwards he and Kristina stayed for drinks, where a constant stream of colleagues and admirers approached him. Doris had told him I was attending – as though he'd know who I was! – and so I felt I had to take this chance to say hello, and introduced myself adding, 'Doris suggested I should …' He smiled and said, 'Ah yes, I remember her mentioning you.' We chatted about Desmond and he kindly consented to a photo – and that was it for me. My dream had come true, albeit under very sad circumstances.

I felt 7ft tall.

With Bert's book under my belt, a German friend, Oliver Bayan, asked what I was going to write next. Next? I hadn't really thought about writing anything beyond these two books, until, that is, he suggested a book on Roger Moore.

'But he's always refused to support biographies,' I reasoned.

'It doesn't have to be personal, it could be more about his work, and I could help.'

Oliver was a big fan of Roger's films and had collected many of his more obscure films and difficult-to-find TV series.

I thought about it for a while and wondered if we wrote a book of two parts, the first being biographical but restricted mainly to his career, without delving too deeply into his personal life, and the second part a complete and detailed filmography and TV show breakdown, would it work? I put an outline together and pitched it to some publishers. Various rejection letters arrived back saying they didn't think him current enough, or they felt a film-based biography was too slight. Then one publisher asked if he'd support it, and if so, they'd be keen.

I approached Doris, who immediately said, 'He isn't interested in a biography.'

I knew that, but she went on to explain there'd been one written in the 1980s and he'd taken great exception to it.

I didn't push it any further at that point, but a few days later she phoned me up and said she'd mentioned it to Roger. His view was he 'wouldn't object, but wouldn't endorse it'.

Fair enough. That initial publisher drifted away (perhaps realising it wasn't going to be salacious enough) but then, another reply came in from Robert Hale Books. They'd published biographies of Sean Connery and Pierce Brosnan, and liked the idea of another Bond-actor biography. A deal was agreed and a deadline set.

Oliver started compiling the filmography and I worked on the main text. Oliver's first language was German and though his English was good, it was sometimes a bit like reading Google translate and, bless him, unintentionally funny. Still, it was nothing a bit of polishing couldn't sort out.

I contacted a number of co-stars, directors and producers from Roger's career, and they were all hugely helpful and keen to lavish praise – it seemed everyone loved Roger. No one had a bad word to say; not that I was seeking any negative comments.

One of the most charming of his co-stars to talk with was Richard Kiel, who played the steel-toothed henchman Jaws in two Bond movies. He had terrified me as a young child (though admittedly turned into a good guy in his second outing) but was so very lovely to chat with, so erudite and gave me just what I needed in terms of colour and tribute. At the end of our conversation he mentioned he'd written an autobiography and was looking for a publisher; it seems he'd tried several in America without much success. I said, 'Let me have a word with some people.'

I picked up the phone to the publisher of my Pinewood book, Reynolds & Hearn. Richard Reynolds had been an editor at another company, primarily on entertainment books, and had decided to set up on his own – well, not quite on his own as he drafted in one of his past authors, Marcus Hearn, as a partner. Richard had become a friend and we met occasionally for coffee and cakes – he was also a Bond fan.

I mentioned Richard Kiel's book and he said, 'I'd love to read it.' I duly emailed Richard Kiel and put them in touch.

Richard K. was in fact due to visit London a couple of months later and arranged to meet Richard R. at his hotel – though meanwhile Richard R. had read the manuscript and said he'd love to publish it. Richard K. in turn emailed me and said he'd love to meet up and would like to take me to lunch; he'd heard about a new restaurant Roger's eldest son had set up with a friend, called Hush. He suggested we meet there.

We did, and had a terrific lunch which was only topped for Richard and his delightful wife Diane by the appearance of Luisa Moore – though now separated from Roger, Luisa had of course known the Kiels well from their time on set and on location. In fact, Diane went off shopping with Luisa to buy an outfit for her new grandchild.

That day a firm friendship was forged and I became Richard's UK representative. He came over most years and asked that I set some things up for him – book signings, appearances, talks at film shows and dinners – to earn a few quid. On his first trip he made so much money he asked if I knew a bank where he could change it into traveller's cheques. I just so happened to know the manager of Barclays in Soho Square (described as being the 'Media Bank') and he arranged for us to go in one afternoon; he'd set up a room with a desk, coffee, chairs and Richard counted out his cash, which they issued cheques for.

Richard was always very appreciative and generous towards me, and whenever he was in town – even if just passing through – he'd make a point of inviting me to join him and Diane for dinner and to see a show.

One year he was over for fourteen days and I fixed twelve events for him all over the country, and it was tiring enough for me let alone Richard. Being so tall, at 7ft 2in, he found most hotel beds in the UK to be quite small, so I'd always make a point of speaking to the managers to ensure they were king size and above. Once or twice we arrived to see standard double beds and the staff assured us it was 'king size'. Richard would grimace, and say, 'Hey, shall I just dangle my feet out the window then?'

Most of the time they'd realise he was being sarcastic and would switch rooms, though now and again you'd encounter an obnoxious hotelier, but Richard was very calm and would say, 'Would you call the Hilton, make a reservation and explain you're paying as you've mis-sold my room to me?'

They did.

Many more adventures followed with Richard, but meanwhile I had a book to finish. I gave Doris Spriggs another update and said I wasn't looking for an endorsement, but would she do me the great favour of reading the manuscript for any factual errors. She agreed, and duly came back with notes to expand some sections, added anecdotes and made a couple of suggestions – all very helpful.

She must have been relieved at our approach as well as impressed, as she told me she'd chatted with Roger and reassured him it was going to be a very positive and good book.

Doris had worked for Roger since the early 1970s, and I know she was finding some things frustrating – not least the fact that Roger had left Luisa and moved in with Kristina. Her allegiance had always been to the Moore family unit – and that unit consisted of Roger, Luisa and the children. Luisa still phoned Doris and asked her to do a few things, and it caused Doris to feel torn. She told Roger that she felt it was time to retire – but he refused, saying, 'If you retire then that'll make me feel old and I don't want that.'

Although she'd probably chastise me for saying so, she was by then in her mid-70s and whilst she loved working and driving to Pinewood every day, I think she really wanted to slow down. She kept saying, 'I think it's time.' Roger had been encouraging her to get a computer and email, which she really didn't want, and what with Roger's accountant – an arrogant a man as I'd ever met – taking over more and more of the administration from Doris, believing only he could handle it, she'd also felt undermined.

I think it was around September 2001 that she told me, 'That's it. I'm doing it. I've told Roger I don't want to go on beyond this year.'

I felt very sad because I liked Doris hugely, enjoyed our little chats and exchange of gossip, and realised it may mean Roger closing down his Pinewood office.

'Remember I'm available,' I quipped. Doris didn't react.

A few days later she phoned me and asked if I had a few minutes to talk. I was out somewhere in London, but found a quiet corner.

'Roger has accepted I'm leaving. I asked him what he wants to do about the office – close it, keep it open, find someone else? He said he'd like to keep it open and asked if I knew of anyone.'

I knew one of the studio secretaries was looking for a job having been made redundant, and was just about to mention her name when Doris added, 'I've told him there's only one person. You. Do you want the job?'

I nearly fell over.

'Sorry, say that again,' I asked.

'You know the business, you know the fan world, you know about his career, you're loyal, trustworthy and I think you'll do him a lot of good.'

'Yes! Yes! Yes! I mean, yes of course I'd be interested.'

'That's sorted then,' she concluded.

'Doesn't he want to speak to me or interview me?' I asked.

'I don't think he needs to. I've told him all about you. He's read your manuscript and he thinks you'll be perfect.'

Wow.

The next day I popped in to see Doris. She explained some of the workings of the office, what files were where and that aside from some petty cash, all financial matters went through the accountant in Geneva. She then told me how much she was paid, and my jaw dropped.

'That wouldn't cover my rent and living expenses,' I said. 'When did you last have a raise?'

Doris had felt guilty about asking as she'd reduced her hours about seven or eight years earlier to care for her elderly mother and Roger had been very kind, though his accountant obviously saw no reason to offer a raise on the basis she wasn't around the office as much.

In all honesty, I told her I simply couldn't afford to take the job on that salary.

'I'll speak to him,' she said.

A few days later I had a call from the accountant who offered me an extra £30 a week, whilst adding, 'There's nothing to do apart from reply to fan mail, I don't know why he needs a PA.'

What a lovely man he was.

I confessed to Doris that even with an extra £30, I'd still struggle. I wasn't greedy by any means, but I'd been scratching around with writing assignments, a bit of consultancy work and other bits and pieces to get by and I would effectively be taking a pay cut. Okay, I wouldn't have to pay rent on my office any more and okay, he said he'd been happy for me to continue writing during quieter days, but even so ...

Doris said, 'Leave it to me.'

She phoned Roger and said, 'Look you need to give the lad what he needs otherwise you'll lose him. Do you know how much your accountant has offered?'

She told Roger and he seemed shocked. 'And that's a lot more than I get now!' she added. He was mortified.

Roger obviously expected his accountant to take care of his staff, ensuring an annual raise in line with inflation, but that had never happened.

I then received an email from the accountant, offering me quite a bit more – though still not a fortune – adding, 'We'll see how it goes in a year.'

Doris said she'd decided to stay on until the end of the tax year on 5 April, because there was much to sort through and she wanted to leave everything neat and tidy and having those extra four or five months would be time enough to do it all. I felt a bit like the president-elect. I'd been voted into office, yet there was a transitional period to sit out.

I gave notice on my office and began winding up my production company, which had really been costing me quite a bit of money to keep open.

I saw Doris regularly and suggested I might email Roger to say hello. In fact, I sent him a rather rude joke I'd been forwarded, and said, 'There'll be more to come.' It must have tickled him, as he replied saying, 'Welcome aboard and I should hope so.'

His office at Pinewood hadn't been decorated in many years – I'd say twenty. I asked studio services if they'd mind freshening it up and was met by a sharp intake of breath. 'Well we only do that for new tenants now, technically you should pay.' I smiled and said, 'After twenty years don't you think it's only fair?'

The decorator was booked for early April, and actually as soon as he started cleaning down the wall, half the plaster on it fell off! It turned out to be a much bigger job than first anticipated but at least avoided injuring anyone sitting at the desk beneath.

I was extremely fond of Doris and told her we must keep in touch after her retirement. 'It'd be nice, but don't feel you have to,' she said in her own stoic way. Well, we did and do – I still see her regularly and we exchange emails (yes, she finally went all computer savvy) almost daily.

On 6 April 2002, I picked up the office keys and started moving bits and pieces down from my office, and settled into Roger's ground floor room with its two desks – one for me, one for him – with just a few photos on the wall. I thought I'd brighten it up with some more photos and posters from his various films so that there was no mistaking it was his office.

I set up a new email account and website domain, and when I picked up the post that morning there was a letter from an Italian TV company inviting Roger to take part in a chat show, offering a sizeable fee.

Doris told me that she'd always waited for Roger to phone in, and would run through any matters of the day and ask any questions she needed answers to – that way she was sure they'd always speak when Roger wasn't busy doing something and she had his full attention. She'd only really phone him with anything urgent, or otherwise send him a fax.

So, on that first day, I awaited his call.

I guess it was about 10.30 a.m. when the phone rang and his dulcet tones wished me a good morning, before he said, 'You'll find it busy at times, and quiet at others. There are occasionally some offers, but not very often, and you'll need to liaise with Jean [his agent, Jean Diamond]. You should introduce yourself to UNICEF and did Doris leave you the list of people to advise of my schedule?'

The list was mainly fax numbers of his children, his agents in the UK and USA, his publicist Jerry Pam, and his stepchildren; whenever he was travelling I was to let them know where, when and how to reach him. Of course, he had a mobile phone, but it'd often be easier to leave any (non-urgent) messages or a fax at the hotel if he was working or travelling with UNICEF.

'Actually an offer came in this morning,' I explained, and read him the Italian letter.

'Ahhh. I hate Italian TV shows. They go on forever. I haven't really got anything to talk about ...'

'They say it's a general career interview.'

'Even worse!' he exclaimed.

'There's a fee,' I added.

'How much?'

It was twice my annual salary, but he wasn't swayed.

'Would you write and thank them most sincerely, but say my schedule doesn't permit? Enjoy settling in and give me a shout if there's anything else. I'll leave you to your day.'

I guess we'd been on the phone for ten or fifteen minutes and it seemed like a good day's work done. So I carried on putting up the photos and posters, before making a few calls to his agent, UNICEF, his regular driver, his regular hotel, the lady who always met him at the airport, his travel agent and so on, just to introduce myself. Everyone was so warm and so welcoming and told me how delightful Roger was.

That first day zipped by and I felt really, really happy and looked forward to work again the next day.

CHAPTER 5

BONDSTARS

Richard Kiel had invited me to the US book launch of his autobiography, which he'd titled *Making it Big in the Movies*. It was at the end of April 2002 at an exclusive address in uptown New York City, at the home of Bob Guccione. Richard also asked that I bring my mother and nephew who I'd told him about during our lunch in London. He was very thoughtful like that.

Bob was the founder of *Penthouse* magazine and was engaged to Richard's niece, April, and that's how Richard knew him. Richard told me it was one of the largest private residences in Manhattan with thirty rooms, its own elevator, indoor pool and an amazing gold piano in the lobby that once belonged to Judy Garland. It was decorated beautifully and I think pretty much everyone stood open-mouthed when they walked in for the first time.

'When people think he founded *Penthouse*, they think he'd live somewhere tacky,' Richard said to me, 'but quite the contrary eh?'

Richard had chosen this particular Thursday evening to have a book party because the next day, for the whole weekend, he was a guest at the huge Chiller autograph show across the water in New

Jersey; the Bond line-up also included Maud Adams, Lois Chiles and George Lazenby, who all attended Richard's party. I chatted briefly to them all, but only really to say hello and mention I was working as Roger's PA. I knew Maud had always been one of Roger's favourite co-stars, from two of his Bond movies. He told me, 'She was always on time, knew her lines, was a delight to work with … and the only one of my leading ladies to make two.'

The champagne continued to flow until late evening, the canapés were delicious and Bob Guccione was a charming host – he even put together goodie bags including a copy of Richard's book and a trademark *Penthouse* cigar for us to take away. Richard Reynolds was in attendance, as fortunately his in-laws lived upstate, and he and Richard Kiel discussed a launch in London later in the year, when Richard was due over for an autograph event. I joined in the conversation and mentioned I could help set some gigs up and, ever the businessman, Richard K. pulled me to one side and said, 'The book retails for about £15, I can buy them in at 60 per cent discount which means I make about £9 per sale plus a royalty. If I sell them for £15 signed, I can do a deal for a book and signed photo for £25 and that's nearly £19 pure profit.'

I suggested the *Memorabilia* show at Birmingham's NEC would be a good show to attend, and Richard then suggested it to Maud, Lois and George.

That year, 2002, marked the fortieth anniversary of the Bond series and there was a new film premiering in November – Pierce Brosnan's fourth – *Die Another Day*, and as the NEC show was scheduled a week before the premiere I suggested we might fill that week up so Richard and the others could stay on. In fact, along with the NEC, I organised for them to attend the official '40 Years of Bond' BAFTA tribute, the premiere, a couple of private evenings in London, and in association with MGM home video had arranged some press gigs in London, Paris and Hamburg – for a little 'consideration'. Tacked on to those there was a shop in Paris and show in Hamburg we could tie in with too for a visit to sign autographs. It was a fun and very profitable couple of weeks.

At the end, George turned to me and my friend Andy Boyle who'd helped me out, and said, 'I've got these photos left over. They're quite heavy. If I signed them and left them with you do you reckon you could flog them?'

We said, 'Yes, definitely.'

'Okay, give me half and we'll do that. Shall I ask Maud and Lois too?'

So we had a couple of hundred signed photos and said, 'We need a website.' Soon afterwards we launched www.bondstars.com as the stars' official autograph portal, and more and more Bond alumni joined; it's still going strong with almost 100 now listed.

Meanwhile, back in London in 2002, Roger was proving to be in great demand for all things 007 as the anniversary of the series approached. Without wanting to be mercenary, he did feel that if he had to go out of his way, then it should be worthwhile. He was always happy to talk Bond, but flying in and out for TV shows and the like was another thing altogether. Plus, Roger always enjoyed earning a few quid.

People used to say to me, 'Surely he doesn't NEED the money?'

Well, actually, yes he did and he also liked being able to still work and earn money; he had earned well whilst he was 007 but post-Bond his movie work took second place to his UNICEF work, and with two homes, three children and several grandchildren, plus a couple of housekeepers and my modest salary, there were a lot of monthly outgoings. Roger didn't live an over-extravagant life but he liked to be able to suffer in comfort. He certainly knew and appreciated the value of money, and I remember he once flew in from Nice where the temperatures were in the high 20s centigrade, into a chilly London struggling to hit 10°C, wearing only his blazer.

'It's okay, I'll buy a new overcoat,' he said.

A couple of hours later, he called me from his hotel which was adjacent to Harrods.

'I've been in looking at overcoats,' he said. 'Do you know how much they wanted for one off the peg in there?'

'No?' I replied.

'Two thousand fucking quid!'

'Did you get a couple?' I asked mischievously

'I bought a fucking scarf – £19.99!' he chuckled.

You might think it was out of character for Roger to swear; it's true, he was always very careful in public and on TV – ever the perfect gentleman – but in private he would 'eff and blind' a bit, but only ever in good humour, and only ever amongst his friends and family.

Whilst appreciating the value of money and always enjoying a good deal, he was also the most incredibly generous person. Whenever there was a charity auction, he'd bid. Whenever there was a fundraiser, he'd send an anonymous donation. Whenever we passed a *Big Issue* seller on the street he'd give them a fiver and say, 'I don't need the magazine, sell it on to someone else.'

When Children in Need asked if he would consider offering himself up for auction with Terry Wogan for a 'lunch with Roger and Terry' he immediately said, 'Yes, but they'd need to know I'm not in the UK a huge amount'. The CIN people said not to worry as they'd aim to get three months' notice of a proposed lunch, and if I could tip them off as to when might work. That event sold for £75,000 – the (then) highest sum ever paid for an auction item on Terry Wogan's Radio 2 programme.

Though as generous as Roger could be, if he ever thought someone was taking advantage of his good nature the shutters would come down instantly. He was no fool.

On 14 October, Roger was to celebrate his birthday – as he did every year! – but this particular birthday was his 75th. He said that he was going to hold a big dinner party at Hush, the restaurant his son

Geoffrey had founded with lawyer Jamie Barber in Mayfair. He faxed me through the guest list and said he'd personally mailed the invitations – he always liked the personal touch – and asked that they RSVP to me to collate.

My name was on the list. I was touched and a little bowled over that he had thought of me.

There were perhaps sixty to seventy people who accepted. It was a really delightful evening and I sat between Deborah Moore and Jean Diamond – Roger's agent – and was warmly welcomed alongside his oldest and dearest friends. It was then I realised you don't work FOR someone like Roger Moore, you work WITH them and are part of the family.

A month or so later, Pierce Brosnan's fourth outing (and his last, as it turned out) as Bond came with *Die Another Day*, and with the Odeon Leicester Square either proving unavailable or too small, the producers announced the premiere of the movie would be at the Royal Albert Hall in London. With it marking the fortieth anniversary of the series, they felt it should also be a massive celebration of the past films and 007s, and duly invited Roger, George Lazenby and Timothy Dalton to join them. Her Majesty Queen Elizabeth II was announced as attending, as Patron of the Cinema and Television Benevolent Fund – the film industry's trade charity which was benefitting from the premiere – and the former Bond actors were invited to join the line-up presented to Her Majesty.

Roger was somewhat upset to be told wives would not be in the line-up, as protocol was such that the queen only ever meets fifteen or twenty people in such circumstances, and with the main cast and crew from *Die Another Day* already nearly numbering that, it wasn't the done thing. Roger told me to say if Kristina couldn't be by his side, then he'd rather not be there. He didn't want to upset protocol, but wasn't about to upset his wife by leaving her in the wings, particularly as he knew she was an ardent royalist.

Word came back that it would be okay for Kristina to stand behind Roger, but I didn't dare tell him that as I knew he'd explode – he rarely did, but certain things really rubbed him up the wrong way and if Kristina was ever slighted, he would just walk away. I just said 'that's fine' and told Roger that Kristina was indeed expected to stand alongside him; I knew no one would dare say otherwise on the night, and let's face it, it would look very odd if Lady Moore was made to stand three steps behind her husband – it was 2002, not 1892.

Though further irritation came when word reached us on the day that former 007s would have to stand in a different room to the present incumbent of the role, as it was suggested the current Bond shouldn't be overshadowed by the past ones. It's not for me to say who suggested it but I think jealousy had a role to play.

It was rather ironic, therefore, after the queen met everyone and took her seat in the royal box, that producers Michael G. Wilson and Barbara Broccoli took to the stage and introduced George, Roger and Timothy – the house erupted when Roger walked on and, without wishing to sound biased, he received a much bigger and longer ovation than Mr Brosnan. Roger always embraced all things Bond, and the fans loved him for it.

Afterwards I told him about the intensity of his applause, and he said he wasn't aware at the time but added, 'Rightly fucking so,' with a raised eyebrow.

It was the first Bond premiere Roger had been to since his last 007 outing in 1985, and he'd never seen any of the subsequent films – bar a reel of *Goldeneye* (1995) which they ran for him during his visit to the set at Leavesden Studios when he popped in to see his son Christian who was working in the location department.

I asked what he thought of the new Bond. He was diplomatically evasive.

George Lazenby was walking out at the same time as me and said, 'I might get into watching Bond films again, that was all crazy.' Just then

Dana Broccoli, Cubby's widow, emerged and saw George. 'Nice to see you've grown up at last,' she said to him, 'and are embracing Bond.'

'I'm not here for you,' he replied, and walked with me across the road to a huge marquee in the park where the party was to take place. Roger and Kristina were flying out the next day and so went straight back to their hotel. I should mention, of course, Roger's daughter Deborah had a small part in the movie as an air hostess, and forever after has been called a 'Bond girl'.

CHAPTER 6

THE COLLAPSE

Roger and Kristina split their year, roughly 50:50, between Switzerland and Monaco. Roger had been a long-time resident of the former, firstly in Gstaad with his third wife Luisa and the family, and then after he split from Luisa and got together with Kristina, they moved to Crans-Montana. Roger preferred life in ski resorts as he was then a regular user of the slopes; he also reasoned good resorts meant there were good restaurants and shops. They settled on Crans after visiting many potential new homes – within easy driving of the airport, but putting suitable distance between them and his former wife to save any potential embarrassment.

Kristina meanwhile had been a long-time resident of Monaco, and prior to that of St Paul de Vence in the hills above Cannes where Roger once owned his South of France summer residence – they were in fact neighbours at one point. Kristina liked Monaco because it was safe – free of crime and major incidents – and though the tax perks were not a primary concern, they didn't harm. She and Roger decided to rent an apartment in the Fontvieille area, which was a whole area reclaimed from the sea, with lots of new apartments, a sports stadium, harbour and shopping. The estate agent had suggested a lunchtime visit to the particular apartment they liked the look of, and sure enough it was perfect, with the added bonus of a lovely terrace overlooking the harbour. 'We'll take it,' they said.

Shortly after moving in, Roger twigged why the estate agent had suggested a lunchtime viewing – at lunchtime the heliport staff went off for the traditional two-hour French lunch break, meaning all helicopter traffic was suspended. As soon as he opened the sliding patio-style windows to the terrace Roger said he was either deafened by the noise of rotor blades, or left standing coughing in the sand and dust storm it stirred up – and not surprisingly, as their apartment was directly above the helipad! They stuck it out for a year or two, and despite only being there for five or six months of the year, they just couldn't bear it any longer, and started looking elsewhere. As luck would have it, an apartment was coming onto the market opposite the Grimaldi Forum, right on the promenade in Monte Carlo. With four bedrooms, two bathrooms and a shower room, a large living and dining room, a spacious kitchen and 24/7 concierge service, it really was ideal. It wasn't cheap, but then again nowhere in Monaco really ever is. Up until Monaco, Roger hadn't really lived in an apartment since his very young days with his first wife, and ever after he'd lived in houses with gardens, though his chalet in Crans had a huge lawn and flower beds – but ironically he was only ever usually there when it was covered in snow.

The split between Monaco and Switzerland suited Roger. In the summer many of his friends, such as Leslie and Evie Bricusse, David Niven, Joan Collins, Michael Winner, Stefanie Powers, Jeremy Lloyd and others, all descended to their summer vacation homes on the Côte d'Azur, and there'd be frequent meet-ups between them all, all along the coast. It was very much a non-stop social club of parties, dinners, receptions and balls. Whereas the winter move to Switzerland, usually in November, was the complete opposite – few celebrities decamped there, which meant Roger enjoyed a quieter time, watching movies, skiing and just enjoying life. He'd often be found in a casual sweater and cords wandering around the local supermarket or bakery, and no one batted an eyelid. He felt virtually anonymous there, which he loved – although he never once refused a photograph or autograph should he be asked.

His chalet was a little off the beaten track, so you'd need to know where you were going. He kept his ever-reliable Volvo 4x4 there, and a little VW Golf that Kristina used to drive. In Monaco he drove a Mercedes, and Kristina an old Golf convertible, but in later years purchased a two-seater Smart car as he complained you could never park the Mercedes in the notoriously small parking bays – that's if you could find a vacant space. The Smart car could literally be parked sideways-on in any little gap.

Roger and Kristina had lunch one day at the Café de Paris in Casino Square, which is always teeming with tourists, and as always he pulled up outside in his car and handed the keys to one of the staff who parked it; you'll find the most expensive cars all parked up outside any time you visit, so it was obviously a great curiosity to see Roger in his tiny two-seater. As he bade farewell to lunch guests Harry and Rita Crosbie and drove off, Harry overheard a British voice in the crowd saying, 'Did you see that? James Bond getting into a bloody baked bean can.' That really tickled Roger when Harry phoned to tell him.

I always got the impression that, as much as Roger loved the Monaco social scene, he was, I think, happiest at home in his cosy Swiss chalet watching TV with his feet up, eating his favourite comfort food: beans on toast. Once upon a time, a move to foreign parts meant he rarely ever saw a pork pie or can of beans, but many French and Swiss shops starting selling British favourites in the 1990s and so on opening Roger's cupboards you would find Paxo stuffing, Bisto gravy granules, and tin upon tin of baked beans. Quite often, if he was about to head off somewhere or to the airport, a quick lunch would consist of a couple of fried eggs, a slice of bacon and dollop of beans – all finished with a big wide smile.

Roger's diary was usually fairly busy up until his annual move to Switzerland, and unless there was an important UNICEF trip, he liked to keep it clear through December and January to just relax, entertain visiting family members, and watch the slew of DVDs the academy (Oscars) sent through to members; sometimes as many as a hundred. The other factor which we had to bear in mind was that Crans is a good two-hour drive to Geneva airport. Add in a couple of hours at the airport to check in, clear security, etc., and it meant they'd need to leave home four hours before any departure; so we always avoided morning flights, and late returns, as you can imagine. Monaco on the other hand is thirty minutes from Nice airport, which made life so much easier, and requests to 'pop to London' for a TV show were considered more favourably when he was in Monaco, and with a slight groan when he was holed up in Crans-Montana.

Although he enjoyed his downtime, Roger was always keen there were some things in the diary later in the spring – he liked to be busy, he liked to work, he liked to feel wanted. In March 2003 there was to be a Broadway engagement for *The Play What I Wrote* and in May some further shows; plus back in London, *Night of 1000 Voices* was scheduled at the Royal Albert Hall, and was a tribute to the musicals of Trevor Nunn, which Roger was going to host.

The Play What I Wrote was British theatre producer David Pugh's West End hit and he was taking it across the Atlantic, and because Roger had starred in a number of performances in London – plus a couple on tour – to great acclaim, he was keen for Roger to be the opening night guest star. However, the powers that be on Broadway insisted it should be an American star for the very first night, but Roger would be fine on night two onwards. There was a bit of a kerfuffle arranging a work visa, and it turned out to be easier if Roger arrived in the country from Canada; in fact, he flew from London to New York and then after a night or two he took a day trip flight up over the Canadian border, processed a bit of paperwork, and then flew back to New York 'all legal'. As the show was based loosely on the comedy of Morecambe and Wise, it was rewritten slightly for American audiences and Kevin Kline became the first night's guest star. Roger then stepped in for three or four nights and toasted his return to Broadway lasting three days longer than his first show there did! Roger hadn't actually appeared on stage for about forty-five to fifty years, and I think the attraction of this show was two-fold: firstly, he didn't have that many lines to learn; and secondly, it was a tribute to Morecambe and Wise whose popular TV show he'd always wanted to appear in, but was never available when they asked him.

A couple of months after his initial Broadway shows Roger was booked to return to New York for another short run in May, and decided to stop in London for a couple of days en route. It meant he was able to take part in a DVD commentary for *The Persuaders!* TV show he'd made in 1971 which was going to be recorded at Pinewood with a couple of his production colleagues. I arrived at the studio early to spruce up the office and Roger phoned me from his car saying he felt he had a cold coming on as his throat was sore, and asked if I could maybe get him some honey to make a hot lemon and honey drink. I must admit he didn't look terribly good when he arrived at the office, but he sat down to sip the hot drink and – ever the pro – said he'd be fine, but just felt a bit tired and run down.

The recording went fine, we then had a spot of lunch and afterwards Roger posed for some photos with the Aston Martin from the series that had been brought in. He said he was going to have an early night back at the hotel with Kristina and would call me from the airport the next day ahead of the flight.

In fact the next morning he said he felt better, and all would be fine – and off they went to New York.

I knew he had a hectic schedule when he landed so wasn't really expecting to hear from him for a day or two – which wasn't uncommon – but on 9 May at around 6.30 a.m. my phone rang. It wasn't Roger, but rather my friend Robin, who asked if I was watching the breakfast news. I wasn't.

'Roger has collapsed on stage in New York and has been rushed into hospital,' he said.

I pulled on a pair of trousers and a sweater, got in my car and made the twenty-minute dash to the office, where I phoned Deborah Moore to see what was happening. She said her youngest brother Christian was out there with Roger, and all she knew was it was a heart issue but he was going to be fine. Within minutes my phone started ringing with the press wanting a comment. Although I didn't know much, my first instinct was to play things down and just say he had been dashing around here, there and everywhere and had simply been suffering with exhaustion and dehydration – all was fine, I said. That seemed to placate them.

I then phoned Roger's agent, Jean Diamond, to fill her in, and next I thought I'd best call Roger's accountant (or 'business manager' as he liked to style himself). It was about 8.00 a.m. by then, and he greeted me with, 'Hello boyo, wet the bed have you?'

It was his rather pathetic attempt at being funny.

'Roger is in hospital,' I replied curtly.

His tone suddenly changed to a very worried one – worried about his client, or his own bank account I wondered? – and he asked what had happened, so I filled him in.

A few hours later Roger phoned. I was so relieved and pleased to hear his voice, though he sounded tired and a little frail. He reassured me he was fine, and that the doctors were wonderful. They'd explained he'd had an arrhythmia, which was an irregular heartbeat, that caused him to black out. They said, 'You need a pacemaker.' Roger suggested he'd speak to his cardiologist in LA and make arrangements. 'No. You need it NOW or you will die,' was the stark reply.

The hairs on the back of my neck stood up as he told me this story. Of course, Kristina was incredibly worried as she'd been there at the theatre – she'd watched his every single performance in the show – and when he collapsed she knew it wasn't part of the act.

That night, after the surgery, Roger and Kristina were due to attend a major UNICEF fundraiser, The Snowflake Ball, and he wanted me to call Mary Cahill at UNICEF – who was in the Goodwill Ambassador Department – to explain what had happened. He said he would still attend, but it would only be a brief appearance as he was to be the first Audrey Hepburn Humanitarian Award recipient and didn't want to let people down. I asked if he was sure, and he said yes, the doctors had agreed he'd be fine but not to overdo things.

He then went on to say, although a bit groggy from the anaesthetic he felt so much better and, with hindsight, realised he had been getting out of breath walking upstairs, and feeling increasingly tired because his heart wasn't pumping correctly. Roger said he must have been talking about UNICEF in his drugged-up state because afterwards his surgeon came to see him and handed him a very sizeable cheque.

'For UNICEF he said … it would have been four times as much if I'd have been a Beverly Hills doctor.'

Even in illness Roger never stopped raising awareness and funds. I later learned Roger had collapsed in the final sequence of the play, and naturally they brought the curtain down but after a few minutes getting himself together he insisted they should finish the show. The production reluctantly agreed and meanwhile called paramedics to attend to him as soon as the performance ended; they in turn took him straight to hospital and said had it happened whilst he was on a plane or in the middle of a UNICEF trip in some far-flung corner of the world, he wouldn't have survived – his timing, if there is such a thing for a heart episode, was perfect.

Not long after Roger returned home we were approached by a small charity called STARS: Syncope Trust And Reflex anoxic Seizures. They asked if Roger would help increase awareness of Syncope – the heart condition his new pacemaker was keeping under control. Also known as 'the blackout trust' its founder, Trudie Lobban, started the movement in 1993 when a family member had been misdiagnosed. It wasn't unusual for Roger to be approached; when it became known he'd suffered with prostate cancer in the 1990s he was continually asked to be a spokesman for various cancer causes and, with the best will in the world, he always declined. It wasn't something he wanted to relive on a regular basis and besides, his energies were all focussed towards UNICEF. However, something struck a chord with Roger and this particular charity – he himself brushed off his attack as a bit of a funny turn, but syncope, if not diagnosed quickly and treated accordingly, can be deadly. Roger asked me to write back and say he was willing to lend his name as a patron and support them verbally whenever possible, but cautioned he wouldn't really be able to attend conferences and events. Trudie was over the moon and soon after I arranged for her to meet Roger, and he also recorded a 'know your pulse' video for them – still on their website to this day – where he explained an erratic pulse is the first sign of a problem, and showed how to take a pulse correctly.

It was all brought home to me a short time afterwards when I bought a poster on eBay. The seller lived a few miles from Pinewood and so I opted to collect in person to save any potential damage in the mail. On arriving I was invited in, and whilst the seller nipped upstairs to bring my poster down, his daughter started chatting about films. I mentioned I was based at Pinewood, and she asked what I did. Somewhat reluctantly I said I worked for Roger Moore. She leapt up and hugged me; 'He saved my life,' she said.

She went on to say she'd suffered a couple of 'funny turns' where she'd blacked out and had read a piece in one of the national newspapers where Roger was talking about STARS and syncope. She immediately sensed this was behind her own blackouts and went to see her doctor with the article in hand – she was diagnosed and treated.

I felt quite overcome, and her father must have wondered what she'd said to me when he came downstairs to see us both sobbing.

I told Roger, and he said, 'It's all been worthwhile hasn't it?'

CHAPTER 7

KNIGHTHOOD

Meanwhile, Roger and Kristina had stopped off in London after returning from New York, in part to consult with their London-based doctor, and it was when they were on their way to Heathrow, returning to Nice, that I opened the morning's mail. There was an official-looking letter from the Cabinet Office – I had an idea what it was, so opened it carefully and read it through. It stated Her Majesty wished to bestow a knighthood on Roger in her upcoming birthday honours list and asked if he'd let them know his answer as soon as practical, adding it was strictly confidential.

A few minutes later Roger called to say they were all checked in and waiting in the airport lounge. I asked if he could be overheard and I could immediately sense a worried tone develop in his voice.

'Why?'

'I need to tell you something, it's very confidential,' I explained.

'Go on …'

'A letter has arrived, saying they'd like to offer you a knighthood.'

'Really?' he asked.

'Yes, really.'

He was quiet for a few seconds.

'They would like an answer – yes or no. Perhaps you'd ask Kristina how she feels about becoming Lady Moore?'

There was a joyful leap in his voice as he turned and spoke to Kristina.

'Well, would you mind replying and explaining we're travelling but would be honoured and humbled.'

'Sure.'

'And would you fax me through the letter as I never know if you're winding me up …!' he concluded.

He of course knew I wasn't.

'I so wish my parents were here,' he added, before saying he had to go as they'd been called for the flight.

Roger did actually have a stepmother. After his mother passed away in 1985, Roger's father – George – became a prime target for 'all the old widows and spinsters in Frinton' who 'circled like vultures around my father', as Roger put it.

Poor George couldn't even so much as boil an egg, and so having kindly neighbours fuss over him was undoubtedly a great help. However, one in particular – Alice – decided she wanted to be more than just a helpful friend who popped in occasionally, and persuaded George it would be for the best if she moved in with him – swiftly adding, 'but I couldn't do that unless we were to be married of course'.

Soon enough she got her way and became Mrs Alice Moore, self-styled stepmother of 'Mr Roger Moore, the actor' – Roger hated hearing her Scottish voice on the phone enquiring, 'Where is my stepson today?'

After his father died in 1997, Roger never saw Alice again although he did always make a point of sending her a Christmas hamper – as he did most of his cousins, aunts and uncles. Once Alice learned I'd taken over the Pinewood office, she phoned me regularly to try and glean some gossip and one of her first calls was to tell me she didn't like the hamper of goodies Roger sent. She told me that she would much prefer some wine instead, and gave me the exact name and vintage of the bottle she enjoyed and suggested a case of twelve would be suitable.

I told Roger and he was really furious, calling her an ungrateful so-and-so. Alice knew he didn't like her, and so didn't waste her time trying to call him – she instead focussed on me. She was perfectly charming, though I sensed an underlying frustration that she was never included in any Moore family activities, and so she switched on a full charm offensive.

'Tell me Gareth, have you ever been to Frinton? Would you like to come and visit me, and have lunch? I do have a lovely bungalow, and you'd be welcome to stay.'

This was all ammunition to Roger, who decided she'd be perfect girlfriend material for me.

'Look, I don't mind if you want to take a couple of days off,' he said, 'nip round and give her one, though be careful of the wig!'

'Wig?' I asked nervously.

'She's bald as a coot, and has the most ridiculous, ill-fitting wig you'll have ever seen,' he explained, 'so be careful not to pull it off when you grab for something in that moment of ecstasy.'

Even though he blatantly hated her, he always enquired after Alice. 'How is your sweetheart?' he'd ask. 'Did you pop round at the weekend for a bit of fun?'

In the run-up to Christmas 2003 he sent me a card, congratulating me on our upcoming wedding day, saying 'F-ing Good Luck, You'll Need It' and enclosed a little Christmas bonus. Later there was also a postcard from Canada mentioning the wig – which he was adamant she'd leave me in her will – and over time similar suggestions via email and notes.

I decided to get my own back on him. On his next London trip I sent him a paper schedule – as I always did – to his hotel for arrival, along with fan mail to be signed. There were visits to his tailor, his barber, the UNICEF offices, dinner with friends on various nights and a single entry one day simply saying, 'Lunch with Alice', midway through his stay.

He didn't say anything on arrival, nor in the days that ensued. However, on the night before the timetabled lunch he phoned me at home, with panic in his voice.

'Who the hell is Alice?' he asked.

'Your stepmother,' I replied helpfully.

'You're not seriously suggesting I'm meeting her tomorrow …?'

'No, it'll be *us* both. Alice and I have something to tell you,' I added.

He paused for a moment and sought reassurance:

'You're winding me up, aren't you?'

'No. I've grown very fond of dear Alice and I guess it'll mean you'll in fact become my stepson.'

He was silent for a second or two and must have heard me snigger.

'You bastard. I nearly fell for it. Speak to you in the morning.'

Roger took things easy for a few months, enjoying the summer in Monaco with frequent trips out on his little Sunseeker boat. He kept it moored in Cap D'Ail – just over the French border – which was a fraction of the price of a mooring in Monte Carlo. He told me the 30ft long boat was about the biggest you could own and captain without the need for a crew to run it. Kristina had bought him the boat for his birthday one year, after they'd spent a happy summer the year prior with Evie and Leslie Bricusse on a hired vessel.

If the weather was fine, and the sea calm, they would head out along the coast and anchor off Villefranche for a swim, and then call a favourite restaurant in the harbour who'd send a little tender to collect them. I once spent a day on the boat with them, and really did feel like a film star!

Though as June came around, Roger started to worry about his knighthood.

'I've not heard anything else about it, do you think they've changed their minds?' he asked me.

I laughed.

'Well they did with John Mills you know,' he added worriedly. Apparently John Mills had received the same type of letter some decades earlier and despite it saying he shouldn't tell anyone, it seemed his wife was so excited that she made a booking at their local restaurant under the name of 'Sir John and Lady Mills' along with one or two other similar indiscretions, ahead of the honours list being published. When the said list was published, there was an omission – Sir John. Or so Roger told me.

I reassured him that there wasn't anything to worry about, and I was right – the day prior to the birthday honours being announced, the palace obviously send an embargoed press release to the media, as the phone started ringing off the hook. Request after request came in from TV, radio and newspapers all wanting to bag an interview to publish/broadcast the next day with Roger's reaction. I suggested to Roger that we pick one or two, and then put a statement together to publish on his website at midnight, which other media outlets could then pick up on. He accordingly spoke to BBC news on the telephone and to *The Times* newspaper, who also sent a photographer over – Roger agreed to do a few shots in the Japanese Gardens opposite his apartment block.

'I needn't have worried,' he chuckled to me at the end of the day. A day later his friend David Frost called and asked him to be part of his Sunday morning chat show, *Frost on Sunday*, to talk about his knighthood and UNICEF – it was, after all, awarded for his charity work.

The birthday honours were announced in June though the actual ceremony usually followed a few months later. 'I hope they do me quickly, I'm knocking on, you know,' he said. He was mindful that his old friend Stanley Baker had been awarded a knighthood but died before he could be ennobled at the palace.

Within a few weeks, we were offered a few dates – Roger chose the first, on 11 October. Fortuitously his sometime Bond collaborator, production designer Ken Adam, was awarded a knighthood in the same honours list and he chose the same date to visit the palace.

Meanwhile, during the summer Geoffrey and his family would usually visit Roger (for Geoffrey's birthday) and spend some time in Monaco, and Deborah would generally fly in for a week too. Christian was then based in LA, working as a TV and film producer, so wasn't a frequent visitor to Europe.

There were 'bits and pieces' – some interviews for UNICEF, some general interviews with journalists who were intent on asking far-reaching, different questions to the 1,000 other interviews Roger had done over his career, but usually ended up with fun showbiz tales instead. Roger never really gave an interview; he just chatted and told anecdotes. So whenever requests came in from magazines, websites and papers about 'a life and career feature', he'd say, 'Oh really?' It would get pretty boring for anyone answering the same questions – who is your favourite Bond girl? What was your favourite Bond gadget, etc.? – and when I headed off quite a few of these requests by saying, 'Sorry, he's not doing interviews at present,' I'd invariably be met with a 'Why?' I couldn't say, 'Because he finds it tedious, boring and would rather watch TV,' so I would say something like, 'He prefers to talk about a new project or trip, but there's nothing happening at the moment.'

Some journalists would persist, thinking I was just being awkward and getting in the way, but my job was to shield Roger from unnecessary intrusions, and I knew when and when not to pass it over to him. Yes, if it was a big feature in the *Sunday Times* of course I'd ask him, but if the *Bridlington Gazette* wanted to do a story for their weekly film column, I knew I was pretty safe in making a judgement. Roger trusted me and never once questioned why I'd turned anything away. I'd sometimes mention them in passing if it was a quiet day, and he'd just say, 'Thanks … anything else new?'

I know some people hated me for shielding Roger from them, but isn't that the job of a PA who is on very good terms with their boss and knows how they think? Does a bank manager's assistant ever get treated with contempt if a journalist is told he's not doing any interviews, or can't be disturbed at present?

As October drew nearer, Roger's son Geoffrey and his business partner Jamie Barber were putting together final arrangements to launch a new restaurant. They'd already established Hush in 1999, in Mayfair, and had decided to take over an old bank in St James's and open Shumi – an oriental fusion restaurant. They suggested it as a venue for a post-palace party for Roger.

Around this time, an actress friend of mine, Eunice Gayson, had called to say she was involved in a Manchester children's charity fundraiser, and they were holding a Bond Ball – she was the first ever Bond girl in *Dr No*. She was hoping to track Sean Connery down to sign a picture that could be auctioned on the night and asked if I knew how to get hold of him. I did actually have a London address for him but didn't know if he was in the country – so I just popped a letter in the mail, explaining, and asked if I could put Eunice in touch. A week or so went by, and I'd popped out for something one lunchtime, and when I returned the lady who manned Pinewood's switchboard buzzed through to say Sean Connery had been trying to get hold of me. I must have laughed or something, as she said, 'Really, there is no mistaking his voice, it's him.' She gave me the number he left, and I called it – it was indeed Sean himself, and he said he didn't mind if I wanted to send something but to make sure there was a stamped envelope inside to return it. Ever the careful Scot.

I told Roger, which gave him a laugh, but he then asked if I knew whether Sean was in town for long. I suggested Roger call him, as he was keen to invite Sean to his little party. I say little – there must have been at least a hundred expected!

On the day of the knighting itself, Roger was thrilled to hear it would be the queen at the investiture. Kristina, Geoffrey and Deborah joined him – Christian was still in LA – and afterwards they had a small family lunch at the Ritz hotel; in fact a good friend of theirs actually arranged a suite for them to stay in for the duration of their visit as a gift.

The evening party was star-studded: Michael and Shakira Caine, Joan Collins, Leslie and Evie Bricusse, Bryan and Nanette Forbes, Barbara Broccoli ... and Sean Connery; considering he and Barbara didn't really get along, as Sean had a long-time view that he deserved more money out of the Bonds, Roger diplomatically seated them a few tables apart. I sat near Michael Winner, who I knew, and was a great raconteur.

Making my way out after the party, I noticed Sean Connery standing by the door. I went over to introduce myself and to tell him we'd spoken recently regarding Eunice.

'Oh hi. Sorry I've just had my eyes done,' he said as he slid on a pair of darkened glasses. 'Could you do me a favour?'

'Erm. Well, yes ...'

'Could you nip out and hail me a cab please?'

How could I refuse?!

There were a couple of photographers present for *Hello* magazine. They'd approached Roger for an exclusive feature about his knighthood; he said yes, but added rather than pay a fee to him he'd like them to come to Shumi to take snaps, and that mention Shumi as much as possible – great publicity for a restaurant about to launch.

A friend of Roger's suggested he should now look into getting a coat of arms. British heraldry is administered by the College of Arms, so I put a call through. They explained that they would spend some time researching Roger's background, to gain an insight into how various elements could be reflected in his arms, which would culminate in an hour-long chat with him. The chap I spoke with sounded rather excited actually, though he took the wind out of my sails when he mentioned the fee – but Roger seemed to think it was worth it, as it would be his one way of 'swanking' on official letterheads and the like. Roger was never really a show-off, but he was obviously very proud and thrilled, and continually said in interviews his one regret was that his parents were not around to be part of it all.

The particular King of Arms assigned to design Roger's crest was terribly jolly and enthusiastic – if perhaps a little star-struck – and spoke to me at length over several phone calls ahead of speaking to Roger directly.

'I think I have a new fan,' was Roger's flippant way of telling me their conversation had taken place. In fact they spoke for well over an hour – Roger mainly listened, he assured me. I can't recall exactly how long it was before Roger was sent what you might call the draft; the King of Arms was keen to point out he'd incorporated yellow and blue, being the colours of the Swedish flag, to involve Lady Moore. Moorhens featured prominently too.

The coat of arms and patent were on vellum, signed and sealed. It was a beautiful thing to behold – but how to frame it? The vellum was not to be pierced, nor stuck down with any form of glue. Furthermore, it needed to be in a sealed frame, preferably with an anti-fade coating on the glass.

I located a specialist framer in Pimlico – the frame costing almost as much as the arms themselves – and then of course Roger asked how I was going to get it over to him, in Switzerland. In short it needed to be crated and shipped with the utmost of care. Roger hung it in pride of place in the chalet – not so obvious as to try and impress visitors, but central to the whole living area. That, and a photo of him kneeling before the queen, were really the only indulgences Roger allowed himself to show off, as all his other awards and trophies were up in his study. He'd always laugh when he invited me up to that room, warning me it was a mess. Mess was not the word I'd use – it was a disaster area. Piles of paperwork, discarded mobile phone chargers, photographs, pens, batteries, books, CDs … all scattered. You'd literally have to move piles of papers off the printer to be able to use it, ditto the scanner. Whenever the phone rang he'd invariably have to move something to find it. For someone so very particular about his appearance and dress, you'd think he'd be equally particular about his office. But no! We were looking for something one day, and there were letters and bills from a decade earlier which he'd dealt with but not thought to file or throw away. I suggested we get a few big black bags, sweep everything into them and leave him with a clear desk, reasoning that he wouldn't miss any of it as he didn't know what much of it was anyway.

There were also bits of notepaper pinned up with various passwords – email, Skype, British Airways executive club and so on. Though they were invariably out of date, as whenever he moved to Monaco for the summer he'd forget what they were and reset everything. He'd occasionally email me passwords and say, 'Keep these safe,' though whenever I offered one up to try he'd say, 'No that's the old one.'

Roger loved technology though. He had always been the first in the queue to buy new things – pagers, fax machine, computer and then later, laptop, an iPad, iPhones and so on. He converted me to using Skype too – primarily because he loved anything for free, and free phone calls were a great idea he thought. Off I went to buy a webcam and he called me up daily – multiple times even – and his voice would boom out of my computer. One day a FedEx driver turned up with a parcel just as I 'connected' with Roger and as he saw me talking to someone, Roger enquired, 'Who have you got there?'

'FedEx.'

'Are they bringing me some dosh?' he asked.

I beckoned the delivery guy to the computer, and as luck would have it, he was a Bond fan. Roger chatted with him for a couple of minutes and the guy almost danced out of the office not quite believing his luck.

On another occasion, when Roger was in Monaco, we were chatting away – often for fifteen or twenty minutes – and at the exact moment Roger drew a breath, his son Christian arrived and obviously he didn't twig we were 'live' either.

'Hi Dad. I'm off to London this afternoon, you wouldn't happen to have a bit of sterling knocking around, y'know, for me to tip?'

'Sure,' Roger replied, 'how much?'

Christian thought for a moment. 'Oh, £500 should cover it.'

'FIVE HUNDRED?!' exclaimed Roger. 'Who the fuck are you tipping?'

Speaking of Skype, it was at one of Roger's birthday dinners, at a now closed Danish restaurant in Knightsbridge, that I first met Janus Friis. There were maybe fourteen of us; I remember Michael Winner being there, Leslie and Evie Bricusse, Bryan and Nanette Forbes and Joan Collins with husband Percy Gibson who, on arriving, said, 'Look at Joan's new wig, isn't it great?' and young Christina, Lady Moore's daughter, arrived with a rather dressed-down young guy, who seemed incredibly shy. None of us really knew who he was, aside from being called 'Janus'. Christina later told me he'd invented Skype (later sold it to eBay for $2.6 billion).

Janus was a very nice guy once you got to know him and very generous to good causes. He was particularly kind to me when Kristina was to celebrate her 70th birthday. She'd chosen to spend it in Dubrovnik, where Roger had been invited to narrate *Carnival of the Animals* for his friend Julian Rachlin – Julian staged an annual chamber music concert in the city, and still does.

Roger asked if I would be free to attend – of course I would be! He suggested I buy a couple of tickets for myself and his daughter Deborah, in order that we could fly out together. No sooner had I looked up times and prices than Roger called me back. 'Don't bother,' he said, 'Janus has offered you both go with him on his private jet.'

I think I'd only ever flown business class once – and that was because a friend had a freebie ticket he gave me – so the idea of flying in a private plane was like nothing I'd ever expected or experienced. Boarding through the executive jet area at Luton airport, where I only needed to turn up twenty minutes before departure, I was driven directly to the awaiting plane and off we went. Similarly, upon landing, a car awaited and after quickly flashing our passports to the waiting officials you zoom off without worrying about the queues, whether your bag will arrive or if you might be lucky to get the next bus out.

What a weekend and what a way to arrive!

CHAPTER 8

KIPLING

Roger had always admired Rudyard Kipling's writing and 'If' was his particular favourite poem, which he read at family christenings and weddings. I remember it because there was a guest house literally just down the road from Pinewood called the Pleasant Cottage, where I'd sometimes stayed, and the owner Mick Butcher had a large mirror in the dining room with 'If' and the subsequent poem painted very elegantly on it – 'You'll be a man my son' are words I always associate with a good English breakfast!

Speaking of Mick, I can best describe him as a very jolly cross between Lurch – the butler of the Addams Family – and Victor Meldrew. He could look very forbidding when he came to answer the front door, and if he didn't like the look of the prospective guest would just say, 'Fully booked,' and close the door in their face. Quite often it would be because they had muddy shoes on, or if they'd dared to ask, 'How much do you charge?' as their opening greeting.

He'd happily get up at 5.00 a.m. and cook you breakfast if you had an early start, but if you asked for any variation to the double egg, bacon, tomatoes and beans on offer he'd be most miffed. If you just asked for tea and toast he'd think you were ill. Mind you, one regular dared to ask him if he could maybe do sausages for a change. 'Sausages? This ain't a bleedin' hotel. I'm stressed enough cooking as it is and only started serving tomatoes and beans as a favour to a guy who lived here for a year whilst at Pinewood, and that made a rod for my own back,' he explained earnestly.

One particularly morning, when I'd stayed there, I went down for breakfast to see Mick coming in through the front door carrying a spade.

'I had to scrape that dead fox up off the road,' he said matter-of-factly to the assembled diners, before telling me he had a letter he wanted me to read. It was from a couple who had stayed the week prior, for a wedding anniversary weekend trip to nearby Windsor. They were grumbling, having requested a double room, that Mick had put them into a twin for their 'special weekend'.

'They never said anything when they arrived and I showed them up,' Mick said, 'yet they claim I spoiled their whole weekend and they want a refund.'

'Will you reply?' I asked.

'Oh yes. I'll tell them, married or not, I don't allow hanky-panky under my roof and they should be bloody grateful I let them be in the same room. Ha, ha, ha.' With that he went back to the kitchen and delivered me a full breakfast – whether I wanted it or not!

But I digress.

In the summer of 2004, Roger and Kristina lunched with their friends Lord and Lady Saatchi in the South of France. Josephine was a wonderful Irish lady, with an enchanting turn of phrase, and a powerful force in publishing and writing. She had recently established a 'Poetry Hour' at the British Library with the aim of 'matching leading actors to programmes of the greatest verse'. Naturally, she asked Roger if he would participate in the future, and naturally he replied '… if I can read Kipling'.

They agreed to a date in October when Roger knew he'd be in London. Whenever he could, Roger loved being in London for his birthday – 14 October – as it was a chance to get together with his mates. His first port of call in town was usually Doug Hayward's shop; Doug had been Roger's tailor since the mid-1970s, along with out-fitting Michael Caine, Noel Coward, Laurence Harvey and Terence Stamp to name but a few. Doug had a couple of well-worn old Chesterfield armchairs where he and his clients would sit to chat – it was more of a social club for many! There Roger would arrange to meet Terry O'Neill, Michael Caine, Johnny Gold and a few others to head off across the road to Scott's seafood restaurant for lunch and a gossip. They were Roger's real mates, and despite often not seeing each other for a year, due to work commitments, they always picked up the conversation where they left off. They called themselves the Mayfair Orphans.

Along with meeting up with his mates, Roger had a few items on the agenda this particular October, including Kipling – for which he and Josephine selected the poems, and Josephine wrote and voiced the introduction and links. I'd never seen Roger quite so nervous as when we arrived at the library on London's Euston Road. The huge building is as impressive as it is daunting and Roger was fearful of letting his literary hero down; he'd never made a secret of being an ordinary working-class boy who didn't have much of an education, due to being moved around during the war, and for him to stand up in the very centre of British literary culture and read was definitely more intense than any film audition he'd ever given.

Roger was very serious that evening. Once pleasantries were out of the way, his normal joking self disappeared. He was now very much in 'Roger Moore – the actor' mode. With his rich, smooth voice he delivered seven or eight of Kipling's most famous pieces, and so focussed was he that he never heard – and hence couldn't correct – Lady Saatchi introducing him as having starred alongside

Sean Connery in the big screen adaptation of one of Kipling's most endearing stories, *The Man Who Would Be King*.

'Did you not hear that?' I asked him afterwards.

He shook his head.

The relief of finishing and receiving a standing ovation was something Roger did hear, however, and afterwards over drinks he said, 'Of course I'd be happy to do it again …' As he said it, he looked at me, raised an eyebrow and shrugged his shoulders as if to say, 'I know, I know … but what can I say?'

A few days later Roger was to be subject of a film retrospective at the Barbican Centre. Film programmer Robert Rider had long been keen to pay homage with a selection of film and TV episodes. I met Robert a couple of times to discuss it all, and there were of course 'must haves': a Bond film, *The Man Who Haunted Himself, The Saint, The Persuaders!* and I also suggested *The Naked Face* – an often overlooked movie directed by Brian Forbes. Roger agreed to attend the opening night, for *The Man Who Haunted Himself* and a post-screening Q&A.

Robert asked who Roger would like to interview him. I suggested he'd always been comfortable with Barry Norman and Michael Parkinson. Whether they proved unavailable (or too expensive) I don't know, but Robert phoned me up and said I had impressed him with my knowledge of Roger's work – well, he was my hero as well as my boss – and suggested I take the stage with Roger. I didn't quite know what to say. I was both flattered and floored. How could I possibly sit opposite Roger, in a packed auditorium, and interview him?

'You'll be fine,' Robert assured me. He then also added, 'There'll be a modest fee too.'

In my best Roger Moore style I asked where I needed to sign.

I was probably running on adrenalin all evening, and vaguely remember we had a dinner beforehand in one of the dining rooms at the Barbican, but all I could think about and focus on was what was about to happen. There were probably more people without tickets than with one in the lobby, all hoping for returns, and Robert suggested we take a back route through or risk spending an hour trying to push through the crowds. Roger took it all in his stride and in good humour, whereas I hadn't really ever experienced anything like it. In writing now, I decided to 'Google' the event in the hope of stirring a few more memories, and found Martin Gainsford's review on one of the leading James Bond fan sites:

Following a very well received screening of *The Man Who Haunted Himself,* known to be one of his own favourites, Sir Roger Moore took the stage to the rapturous applause of the filled-to-capacity auditorium. Accompanied by his PA and biographer Gareth Owen, Sir Roger appeared at ease and comfortable with the audience who sensed they were about to embark upon a very enjoyable journey through an illustrious career. Given his professional position the rapport Gareth enjoys with Sir Roger is unsurprising. Nonetheless the interview was handled magnificently with sensitivity, humour and enthusiasm and for this Gareth is to be heartily applauded. Sir Roger imparted stories from his youth as an evacuee during World War II, as an artist and animator, a soldier, a male model and finally as a struggling extra in the British film industry. His wicked and sometimes bawdy sense of humour peppered the conversation when he mentioned for example the 'short toga and long spear' he sported in a variety of costume dramas. Despite still remaining an incredibly handsome and charming man Sir Roger took every opportunity to mock himself. It is this self-deprecating humour which has served him so well during his lengthy career and it took very little time for the three hundred strong audience to become completely entranced by his very genuine personality.

Given the array of talent with whom he has been fortunate enough to work over the years Sir Roger's skill as a mimic has been honed to perfection and the audience were treated to some remarkable impressions of, most notably, Michael Winner, Noel Coward, Michael Caine and fellow 'Persuader' Tony Curtis. Memories of an amusing incident during the making of *The Man With The Golden Gun* allowed Sir Roger to further regale us with his impersonations of Herve Villechaize and Christopher Lee who, spoofing himself in the role of Dracula, once commanded a group of bats back into a cave when they flew out toward the crew during location filming in Phuket.

With Gareth effortlessly guiding Sir Roger every aspect of a phenomenal career was touched upon from the days of Ivanhoe and Maverick through to his duties as a UNICEF ambassador, a role for which he perhaps displays the most pride. Even his recent health problems were discussed with no small candour yet still Sir Roger joked as he related the frightening story of his collapse on stage during a performance of the Morecambe and Wise tribute production *The Play What I Wrote.*

With the fascinating interview continuing longer than may have been planned Gareth quickly threw the gauntlet out into the audience for a brief question and answer session. Sir Roger fielded admirably everything from 'Did you once live in a house in … (Insert location as desired!)?, to 'Who was your favourite "Bond girl"?' This particular question was handled with perfection when Sir Roger explained that he was too gentlemanly to name one but noted that Maud Adams had indeed appeared with him twice! An interesting question revealed that Sir Roger regards the eccentric hero ffolkes in *North Sea Hijack* as one of his favourite roles. A young lad from the audience was clearly awestruck to actually be speaking to his idol when he asked, 'What was your favourite gadget in the 007 films?' Sir Roger's reply, after first ascertaining the boy's age, was the magnetic watch he had so adeptly used to undress Madeline Smith in *Live and Let Die*. Other interesting anecdotes were shared with Sir Roger offering Ewan McGregor as a potential replacement for Pierce Brosnan in the role of James Bond after having met the Scottish actor who now works himself for UNICEF. A delightful interlude to the session occurred when an elderly gentleman sitting in the best seat in the auditorium, front row centre, suddenly got up and politely explained to Sir Roger 'I'm sorry but I have to leave now.' Sir Roger immediately leapt from his seat, shook the man's hand thanking him for coming and asked his name. The unfazed actor then led the audience in a spontaneous round of applause for the old gentleman who waved back to the crowd and left. Another example of why Sir Roger is so well regarded amongst the show-business fraternity. He really does seem to be a very, very nice bloke.

With the evening coming to a close Sir Roger brought the house down by offering upon the request of a member of the audience one of the most beloved lines in cinema, 'The name is Bond, James Bond.' The audience rose to its collective feet and Sir Roger enjoyed a much deserved standing ovation. A few lucky front row attendees obtained autographs as Gareth and his 'guvnor' left the theatre and then they were gone. Upon leaving the auditorium there were few who were not grinning broadly. We were truly privileged to have been able to share some time with a man who deserves, without question, the mantle legend.

Although Roger was used to reading his own reviews – only if they were good ones, he'd caution – I'd like to think it was my first good notice, albeit shared significantly with the man I came to call 'my co-star'.

In the car back to their hotel both Roger and Kristina said, 'Well done'. With hindsight I should have said, 'How about a pay rise then?'

though I realise Roger would have been as quick-witted as ever and probably have said something like, 'You're lucky to be working at all.'

A few days later we all flew to Dublin for a UNICEF fundraiser. I'd been in contact with the team in the Dublin office on and off for some months, and they kindly extended the invitation to me to join them on the evening – though I should add Roger paid my fare and hotel.

Not only had I shared a couple of experiences with Roger 'on stage' at the British Library and Barbican, I was now being submerged into the other important part of his life too. With charm, passion and unrivalled enthusiasm, Roger held the room – and most were fairly merrily tipsy – in the palm of his hand. People dug deeply, pledged generously and vowed to continue supporting UNICEF in small, and sometimes major, ways.

I witnessed a master at work that night – it was both humbling and joyous.

UNICEF arranged for a lovely driver to look after us, Michael – I'm pretty sure he gave his time and limo for free – and along with being a very good driver, which was always a prime concern to Roger after they'd encountered many 'idiots' over the years trying their best to impress 007 with their driving skills, and on our day off ahead of returning home, Michael asked if he could be of service. Roger was keen to try a seafood restaurant in Dún Laoghaire, Cavistons, but said he'd book a taxi as he didn't want to take up Michael's time.

'Nonsense, I'm at your disposal,' said Michael.

It was a twenty- to thirty-minute drive out of the city to the small shop and restaurant – small, but perfect in every way – and being on a main road with lots of little shops adjacent it was fairly busy, and proved tricky to park outside. Michael said he'd drop us, go off to find a parking space and for us to just give him a call when we'd finished.

'No,' said Roger. 'Drop us off, go and park up and then come back to join us for lunch.'

'Oh no, you don't want me there, it's okay …' Michael started, but Roger interrupted him, 'You'll be our guest — we insist.'

That was Roger all over. He treated everyone the same, and if someone was doing him a good turn he showed his appreciation and wouldn't take no for an answer.

Throughout lunch he and Kristina chatted away with Michael, asking him about his family, his work, his recommendations for places to see and restaurants to visit. They were genuinely interested and it was then we learned Michael gave a lot of his time to UNICEF, and thereafter whenever Roger visited Dublin he asked for Michael to be his driver — and I know tipped him handsomely, and usually took him to lunch.

Kipling featured on and off in Roger's life over several more years too, including another reading at the British Library and later at the Nobel Museum in Stockholm, on the 100th anniversary of the writer receiving his Nobel Prize. More on that later.

The two stars of *The Play What I Wrote*, Hamish McColl and Sean Foley — actually, there was another cast member too, Toby Jones as comic turn Arthur, and Roger was so very delighted when Toby became a film star in his own right — called Roger and said they'd been commissioned to make a comedy sketch show for the BBC, and were putting together a pilot. They obviously wanted to throw everything at it and wondered if Roger would be part of it — along with Dawn French, Daniel Radcliffe, Simon Callow, Will Young, Jerry Hall and others. An all-star cast to say the least. They wanted to film in Switzerland and have Roger play a butler in an exclusive chalet. It certainly had all the potential to be a new Morecambe and Wise style show … and maybe that was the problem? It was perhaps considered to be a pale imitation of the famous duo, and the BBC did not commission a series. The final nail in the coffin came when it was broadcast at 11.30 p.m. on BBC2 – the BBC clearly had little faith in it, which was a shame as it had legs and just needed a bit more time to find its niche.

Roger kept in touch with Sean and Hamish, but then they went on to be successful writers and directors in movies … though never once asking for Roger, which I thought rather sad as he had always made a point of helping his mates out.

In fact, in all the years I was with Roger I believe only Michael Caine ever made a suggestion of 'this could be a good part for Roger Moore' – and that was for a film he was making called *Is Anybody There?* (2008), set largely in an old people's home. It came to nothing, but at least Michael thought of him. Not that Roger was desperate for work, but he obviously did like to be thought of. When his old friend J.J. Abrams was announced as director of *Mission Impossible III* (2006), Roger wrote to congratulate him and said, 'If you ever need an old English fart remember I work cheap.' It was meant as a joke, though I think a tiny part of Roger meant it. J.J. replied saying, 'Oh I'd so love to work with you again …'

But there you go, it never happened – that's showbusiness.

Though I've seen, in many departments across the film industry, how when you're working and successful (and useful to others), the phone always rings; but when people don't see you as being useful any longer, the phone stops. That's true in all walks of life I guess, and don't get me wrong, I'm not saying Roger was ever bitter, but he helped a lot of people get a leg-up, who have gone on to great things, and they never returned the favour.

One old friend who Roger had a lot of time for was Tony Curtis, and when *Empire* magazine contacted us to say Tony was to receive the 'Empire Lifetime Achievement Award' in March, they asked if Roger would consider presenting it. Flights and hotel would, of course, be covered. Roger agreed and we made all the arrangements. *Empire* had booked the Dorchester for Roger, despite the awards being at the

Hilton in Paddington and I remember him calling me on arriving – which he only ever did if there was a problem really.

'What's wrong?' I asked.

'Wrong? Nothing! You should come and see the size of this fucking suite they've given us. There's two bedrooms, a dining room, a kitchen, a sitting room – it's bigger than our damn apartment!'

He made me promise to go up early the next day to have a look, ahead of the awards show. He wasn't wrong.

We were chauffeured by limo to the Hilton, where Roger and Kristina walked the red carpet for all the journalists and photographers, and then into the vast function room. Tony and his wife Jill were there and the two men immediately threw their arms around one another, like long lost brothers. It was lovely to witness.

I found myself sitting on an adjacent table between Leslie Phillips and the writers Neal Purvis and Robert Wade – who'd penned the last couple of Bond films and were at work on Daniel Craig's first one. Leslie told me Roger used to be his understudy in the West End, and the two writers asked if I would introduce them to Roger. I led them over and introduced them.

'Did you write *Die Another Day*?' was Roger's opening question as he shook their hands.

'Yes,' they replied.

'I had to sit through that at the premiere …' he laughed. 'How's it going with Daniel? I think he's going to be very good, but there's a lot of negative press going around …'

They chatted for quite a while as I remember, and they were keen to ask Roger all sorts of questions about his films, his directors, his thoughts on the character and so on.

It was a really lovely evening, though as always with these events the dinner was served at about 10.00 p.m. when we were all ready to go home. After a quick mouthful of the starter our car arrived, so we headed back – though not before Roger and Tony hugged again.

It was truly lovely to see Tony receiving a standing ovation that night and I guess it brought home to me how I sometimes felt Roger never received the recognition he should have.

Roger had no idea, but a little later in 2006 a mate of mine – wine expert Olly Smith – and I were chatting about his impending 80th birthday and how it would be nice – and appropriate – if BAFTA paid some sort of tribute. After all, they were the British Academy and Roger was the quintessential British film star. We'd both been to BAFTA events where they honoured industry legends, and bestowed 'Special BAFTAs', and of course every year at the film awards they presented a fellowship too. We both felt strongly that Roger had contributed a lot to the business and he remained a very passionate ambassador for it, and Bond in particular. I spoke with BAFTA committee member Angela Allen, a script supervisor who was a bit of a legend in the business and who had worked with Roger. She said she'd raise the idea at the next meeting and was certainly very enthusiastic. Roger had hosted the BAFTA awards show in the past and had been a guest host in giving out awards too – he'd put himself out for them.

A few weeks later a very frustrated Angela Allen called me to say she'd tried but the response was of non-interest.

Of course I received a reply to my letter, as did Olly, thanking me for the suggestion and explaining that BAFTA has many people they'd like to honour, and of course it simply wasn't possible to pay homage to each and every one but they would 'bear him in mind'.

BAFTA never did anything – not even a film screening or Q&A in the Piccadilly HQ – to honour Roger turning 80, yet when they were later looking for supporters in fundraising for their headquarter redevelopment, a letter arrived inviting him to make a sizeable donation.

I filed it in the 'non-interest' drawer.

CHAPTER 9

MORE BONDING & KIPLING

In February 2006, the culmination of Hilary Saltzman's efforts to honour her father, Bond co-producer Harry Saltzman, in his home country came to fruition with *Vue sur Bond* in Quebec City. As part of the 3 Americas Film Festival, and supporting UNICEF, Hilary asked Roger if he'd attend. He didn't hesitate to agree, and along with him director Guy Hamilton, Bond girl Britt Ekland, Richard Kiel and Dame Shirley Bassey.

When he arrived in Quebec, Roger phoned to say he'd been on the same flight as Guy (with whom he made two of his Bonds) and apparently Guy said, 'I enjoy emailing Gareth. He likes the gossip doesn't he?'

Bless. Guy was always the one to ask me, 'Any news?'

Roger was later particularly keen to praise Richard Kiel. The group had taken part in a couple of press conferences, and at every stage Richard turned everything around to talking about UNICEF and kept the focus on awareness of the most pressing causes.

Hilary Saltzman and her brother Steven had known Roger since they were young children and had all kept in touch long after their father left the Bond franchise, and despite Cubby Broccoli and Harry parting ways in the mid-1970s, Roger remained loyal to Harry and was always supportive of any projects to help preserve his legacy and memory. The event in Quebec went a long way towards doing just that, whilst also helping raise funds and awareness for UNICEF.

Of course, Roger continued to speak about UNICEF long after he left Canada, and one of his favourite TV chat show hosts in the UK was Paul O'Grady. Roger had guested on his teatime show pretty much every year since it started in 2004, and Paul always made a point of bringing UNICEF into the conversation. In 2006, Paul switched networks from ITV to Channel 4 and again Roger accepted his invitation to chat, twice in fact that year. Paul usually had his dog on the show, Buster, who was a shih tzu-bichon frise-cross; Roger loved dogs and when the family lived in Denham in the 1970s they had a golden retriever who Roger named Greg (after Gregory Peck) and he often lamented to me how he'd love a dog, but his constant travelling made it impractical.

I sensed a true glimmer of regret in his voice, so asked him if he thought he might ever retire, hang up his passport and get a dog. He laughed and said he'd love to though he wasn't sure his bank manager might agree it was a good idea.

'If you ever did, where would you do it – Monaco, Switzerland, the UK?' I asked.

'I've always had this dream I'd retire to a small holding in Kent, with some animals, and stand at the gate watching the world go by. But I left the UK a long time ago, and not by choice.'

'Well, you did have a choice, surely?'

'The thing is,' Roger explained, 'an actor's life – when you're earning good money – is relatively short-lived. For years I scratched around and then had a bit of success, and then when Bond came along I was suddenly earning big money, but also paying big tax. In the late 1970s the Labour government said they were going to squeeze and squeeze the rich "until the pips squeaked" and tax reached 96 per cent. I couldn't afford to stay. I had to think about my future and try and save some money for when the phone stopped ringing.'

'But do you still think of London as your home?' I asked.

'Yes, it's always nice to go back, but I had to make my home and my life elsewhere and I quite like where we are now.'

Of course, whenever I rode in a London taxi with Roger he had a story about virtually every street we drove past, whether it be where he used to buy sandwiches whilst working for an animation company in his youth, to where he auditioned for films, to where he had dodgy agents offer him a contract (only to disappear from the building the next day with a string of debts left behind), to where he enjoyed a 'knee trembler' in a doorway, or even where he used to visit his first (slightly dodgy) tailor: 'Very gay. He used to go to Euston station late at night to pick up any young men who'd missed their last train home and offered them a bed for the night. The dirty so-and-so didn't have any intention of letting them sleep though,' he giggled. Roger literally had a story for every corner – I'm sure the drivers were hugely entertained too.

Roger didn't speak of regrets in his life, as he always maintained he was happy, fulfilled and loved – and wouldn't change a single thing. However, there were moments where he sometimes expressed a tinge of sadness. He always loved talking about Denham for instance, and I sensed it was a period in his life when he was hugely happy in his marriage to his wife Luisa – he was Bond too, the children were growing up and the world was his oyster. Though he'd be quick to add, 'but now I have Kristina'.

If he was talking about times Kristina wasn't familiar with, such as at Denham, he'd say, 'That was BK, my darling – before Kristina.' Both Roger and Kristina had of course lived full lives and had families before they met, so I'd occasionally hear 'BK darling' throughout the years after I started working with Roger, which was as sensitive a way of him talking about his previous wives as possible – no partner wants to be reminded too often of the previous wives or husbands, though equally can't of course just brush them under the carpet.

Kristina never minded any mention of Doorn van Steyn or Dorothy Squires, but if ever Mrs Moore the third, Luisa, was mentioned I always sensed Kristina becoming awkward – slightly tense. It is understandable, as they were once close friends, but you can't always predict how love will work out and how life changes as a result can you?

Bond came around again, as MGM and their DVD distribution partner, Twentieth Century Fox, were set to bring out the 'Ultimate' edition of the Bond films on disc. Extra features including documentaries and commentaries (including seven with Roger) featured, and the studio wanted to make a big splash.

'Would Roger be involved?' came the question.

'Would Roger be paid?' was his response.

All was agreed for Roger to give a day of his time talking to journalists and TV media, and it was all going to be done at the Dorchester Hotel in London. Roger was no stranger to these types of junkets, where he literally sat in a chair for a few hours in front of a pre-lit and pre-set couple of cameras, and journalists were ushered in and out every few minutes, and handed a disc of their interview at the end. Though on arriving at the Dorchester we were told the company had 'two floors' of activity.

'They're spending some money here,' Roger said as we walked down a long corridor packed with camera kit, lights, cables and people buzzing around.

One by one, Roger met members of the press and each asked him about his time as Bond, his favourite films, favourite locations, favourite gadgets and so on. He could have easily looked bored or fed up, but Roger greeted each question as though he'd never been asked it before and made sure every journalist went away feeling happy. I will say, whenever Roger threw himself into doing something, he did it terribly well.

Another invitation, from Lady Saatchi, came for Roger to again read Kipling at the British Museum in October 2006 and again Roger willingly accepted. Less than a year later, another invitation to read Kipling came in, but not from Lady Saatchi or the British Library, but from the Nobel Museum in Stockholm. That year, 2007 marked the centenary of Rudyard Kipling receiving the Nobel Prize for literature and the museum wanted to mark the occasion by having Roger deliver a ninety-minute lecture on his favourite writer.

'What are you doing at the weekend?' Roger asked me one Wednesday morning.

'Well, I was going to visit my mother … why?'

'Would she mind if you went next week, as I'd really like you to come here to Monaco and help me.'

He explained he'd accepted the invitation to go to Stockholm but hadn't really thought about how he would fill the ninety minutes, and had seemingly received some guidance notes suggesting his lecture should be biographical, rather than just a series of poems and it was to be 'ninety minutes exactly'.

'Get one of your cheapo flights, say Friday to Sunday,' he suggested, 'and help me write this lecture, would you?'

'But I don't know much about Kipling,' I protested.

'That's okay, I've got some books here for you. Now, sort that flight. Easyjet is the cheapest isn't it?' he joked.

Easyjet was indeed the least expensive, though by the time I added a taxi – both ends – into the mix, it was very nearly £500 – but with an impending audience of hundreds at the Nobel Museum waiting to hear Roger speak a week later, it was obviously a small price worth paying.

On arriving that Friday evening, Roger suggested I unpack and that we'd go out for dinner.

'What about Kipling?'

'There'll be time for cake later,' he joked. 'Tomorrow.'

We went down into the basement parking lot of the apartment block, and to an old convertible VW Golf. It was Kristina's which she'd owned from new, about twenty years earlier.

'It's easier to park if we take the Golf,' Roger smiled.

My mind went back to the scene in *For Your Eyes Only* where Bond meets Melina Havelock, escaping from bad guys, and she says they can take her car; they turn a corner, and there is a 2CV. Not exactly the speedy powerhouse of a car that was anticipated.

I climbed into the back, and with the hood down, Roger – resplendent in his white linen shirt, white cotton trousers and white loafers – drove us through the narrow streets of Monte Carlo, through various tunnels and into the port. I couldn't help but pinch myself, being driven around Monaco by Roger Moore himself.

I asked him what the difference was between Monaco and Monte Carlo, as they seemed indistinguishable to me.

'Monaco is the principality, or country, whereas Monte Carlo is one of the cities within it,' he helpfully replied.

Quai des Artistes in the port of Monaco was our venue for dinner and we sat outside in the balmy late summer air as a seemingly endless array of seafood – oysters, giant prawns, scallops and more – all came our way. Roger and Kristina always enjoyed white wine, preferably a young Sancerre or a New Zealand, with lunch and dinner; whereas I've never drunk, so that meant all the more for them. Roger always asked why I didn't drink, asking if it was a 'Welsh chapel thing'. Not at all! I've tried the finest wine, spirits, beer … you name it … and it all tastes sour to me.

'It's an acquired taste,' I was often told. Well, I'm sure vinegar is too, but I've no real desire to persist in drinking it until I acquire it.

'The worst thing about not drinking,' Roger mused, 'is that this is as good as you're going to feel all evening.'

'So who needs booze then?' I asked. 'I feel pretty happy.'

Mind you, he did once suggest I try a Limoncello in a restaurant, as a digestif, post dessert. He knew it tasted very sweet and of citrus, so was sure I'd like it. I must admit, a little egg-cup sized glass of it was quite palatable but when a second glass was delivered – much to Roger's delight – it turned my jaw bones stiff with sourness.

They only ever drank white as red gave Kristina a terrible headache, as in fact does Chardonnay – which she tells me is a much heavier type of white wine. I'm afraid it all tastes like vinegar to me … heavy or light.

'You'll have dessert won't you?' Roger asked, as he shoved a menu in my hand. I'd like to think he was just being a charming host, though I suspect he actually wanted one himself and I was to be the reason – he couldn't let me eat alone.

Kristina very rarely, if ever, had dessert. She enjoyed a starter and a main, but aside from maybe a taste of anything Roger had, she always politely declined. I wish I had that same discipline!

The next morning, after some toast and marmalade, Roger laid out the various biographies, books and poetry volumes he owned on Kipling and asked where we should start. I suggested we draw up a timeline of the milestones in his life and career, and a second timeline of when he wrote his poems and short stories. We could then merge the two, peppering and punctuating the biographical stuff with poems. I then asked him to give me a couple of hours alone in his study to come up with the basic outline – though he couldn't resist popping in asking if I wanted a coffee, and how it was all going. We took a break for lunch and had some salad and cold cuts Kristina helped prepare, before standing back and marvelling at the fifty or so pages we'd prepared.

I suggested the only way to see if it worked was for Roger to read it, and we'd time it.

The first run-through took nearly two hours, and as he read through Roger made some notes and struck out a few paragraphs here and there. Kristina kept telling him to pick up the pace, 'otherwise people will get bored' she warned him. She had sat through enough speeches and press conferences in her time to know what kept audiences hooked!

By about 6.30 p.m. we were pretty exhausted.

'Time to freshen up, and then we're out for dinner to Cap D'Ail. Okay?' he asked. 'Restaurant la Pinède, great fish.'

Who was I to argue?

Again we ventured downstairs and into the VW Golf and through Monaco, just over the border into France and the beachside restaurant. Roger recommended the John Dory, with roasted garlic.

'Roasted garlic ... with fish?' I queried.

'Trust me,' he replied, 'it's so delicious.'

Roger had some unusual, or should I say unconventional, but quite perfect dining tips. Once, when my friend Damian and I were at the Cannes Film Festival, Roger invited us over to Cap Martin, on the Italian side of Monaco, for lunch, and when Damian ordered the risotto Roger ordered a glass of Jack Daniels on the side. 'Try it all over the rice,' he suggested. Again, spot on!

Back to la Pinède. There was a quite distinct air of celebration, as Roger had clearly been worried about his Kipling address but was now less so. He suggested, the next morning, we should run through it all again, time it, and for Kristina to make notes about where she felt the pace slipped, or something didn't work. Roger really brought the poetry to life, so it was really more the biographical content Kristina was going to study.

Roger was very relaxed, and had enjoyed a few glasses of the white stuff, and – as always – began regaling us with some of his Hollywood tales.

'Don't you think he should write a book?' Kristina asked me. 'He tells all these stories and I know people would be fascinated.'

'What my darling means,' Roger interrupted, 'is that she is fed up of hearing them so thinks others should suffer instead.'

'No!' Kristina countered. 'Don't be evasive. You really have so many wonderful stories. Don't you agree Gareth?'

'I do. He does.'

'Why do I get the feeling I'm being ganged up on?' Roger asked suspiciously.

'You're not,' Kristina assured him. 'It's just I've seen you and Gareth at work today, and I think you would be brilliant together writing a book.'

'But no one wants to read about me. I'm not a celebrity chef!'

I interrupted, 'There are millions who would love to read your story. You've never told it before and, if I may say so, you're approaching 80 and there's a new Bond film coming out this year, plus another in 2008, which always heightens interest in you — so it's the ideal time to think about it.'

Roger didn't reply. Whenever he knew he was in a corner with no way out, he was quiet. There was no glib or funny remark.

'Do you think it'd pay anything?' he asked.

'Absolutely. Leave it to me and when I get back to London I'll speak with my book agent.'

'Well. What would you like for dessert Gareth?' he asked, proferring me the menu, 'because I can't eat one alone.'

After paying the bill, Roger gave me the car keys. 'Here, you'll have to drive.'

I'd never driven Roger before and although I was and am usually a confident driver, I suddenly felt anything but. I know he and Kristina were nervous passengers, so I didn't dare show any nerves or signs of indecisiveness, and once I'd adjusted my mirrors I started the engine and manoeuvred out of the parking spot slowly, trying desperately not to look as though I was attempting to impress 007 with stunt-driver-like skills. Roger gave directions all the way, and a bit like a driving examiner, at the end congratulated me for a nice smooth journey.

The next morning, after our tea and toast – Roger liked toast with thin peel marmalade by the way, and other than toast sometimes had porridge with a bit of fruit, so breakfast was always usually fairly light and fuss free – we picked up our notes, moved into the sitting room and, as an audience of two, Kristina and I watched and listened to his delivery of the lecture. A few trims here, a little cut there, and by lunchtime we felt we had it. Of course, we broke off for a bite to eat, and then did one final run through before I had to think about packing my bag to head to the airport.

'Can I call a taxi for 4.00 p.m.?' I asked.

'No,' he said, 'we'll take you. I insist.'

This time we didn't pile into the VW Golf but rather Roger's long wheelbase Mercedes, which offered such a beautiful and graceful ride to the airport. All the way there he chatted about his Hollywood friends, regaling me with stories of David Niven and Gregory Peck, and also telling me how upset he was that Dirk Bogarde shunned him – well, it wasn't Bogarde but rather Tony Forwood, his manager and lover (or gardener, as Bogarde often described him) when the duo lived in Grasse. Bogarde had a great disdain for St Paul de Vence where Roger and several of his mates lived, calling it 'Hollywood on the hill', but when Roger learned Bogarde had recommended him for a part he simply wanted to thank him. Forwood answered the phone and said, 'I'll pass the message on.' Roger left his phone number, but never heard back and seemed really saddened. Maybe Bogarde simply didn't want to be involved with the expats on the hill, or maybe Forwood was jealous?

'These will all be good for the book,' I told him.

CHAPTER 10

BOOKS & BOATS

When I returned to London I put through a call to my literary agent, Lesley Pollinger, and explained that Roger was keen to write his autobiography – well, he was as keen as he could ever be.

The non-fiction bestseller list was then, as now, largely occupied by celebrity chefs' books and 'tell all' biographies from the likes of Katie Price and Russell Brand.

'They're all young,' Lesley explained. 'Yes, they're current, yes, they have large fan bases, but they only have twenty years to write about. There is something much more special about a man who has lived for eighty years and never before told his story – it's a real life story.'

I suggested if Lesley could put some feelers out, then I'd arrange for her to meet Roger on his October trip to London to firm things up – I told her he was rather insecure, so best not to share any rejection letters with him, or it'd knock his confidence.

Though, I did warn Lesley that Roger had told me he wouldn't be writing a *News of the World* style 'tell all' book – his private life was just that, and he certainly wouldn't mention any previous girlfriends. Ever the gentleman. Of course, that probably lowered the potential value of the book in some publishers' eyes, and a few dropped out of the bidding.

Within a few weeks, Lesley had assembled a short list and rather than just looking at who might pay the most, she looked at their track records in actually selling books. 'There's no point having a big advance and not seeing anything else down the line,' she warned. 'We want the book to sell, and royalties to continue for years to come.'

Top of the list came Michael O'Mara.

'He sells a LOT of books,' Lesley told me. 'Michael himself doesn't often meet potential authors, but has said he'll come to wherever Roger is if it'll seal a deal.'

Roger arrived in London and met with Lesley. She chatted through the various possibilities and said she'd really like Roger to meet Michael O'Mara, and set up a coffee meeting at Roger's hotel. Within minutes of meeting, I could see (from my far off vantage point) Roger and Michael were getting on like a house on fire – it was reassuring that not only did Roger have a publisher who knew who he was, but was very much on the same page (if you'll forgive the pun) as to the style and feel of book – Michael loved David Niven's books and said if we could capture the fun and essence of those, we'd be onto a winner.

Roger was quite adamant I should be his partner in the venture, his ghost, as it were. I know Roger was conscious of his spelling and grammar, worrying it might prove embarrassing, but I reassured him the way we'd work is that he and I would sit down, chat, and I'd go away to type it up, and then he could tinker. He also loathed the idea of sitting in front of a computer typing page after page!

A deal was agreed, and it made sense to release the book in the summer of 2008 – just ahead of Daniel Craig's second Bond film hitting cinema screens, and thereby allowing us to ride on the 007 press wave. Lesley then set about agreeing deals in other territories, most importantly America, where we signed to Collins (part of HarperCollins).

We had just over six months to come up with a draft, and that focussed Roger enormously – he hated being late for any appointment, so was particularly mindful we needed to get 'arses in gear'.

Having enjoyed many summers on their boat in the South of France, Roger told me in the year or two prior to 2007, they'd only been out four or five times – bad weather, lots of travelling and some time out of the water being serviced and repaired all combined to make trips few and far between. He said it was costing him a fortune in mooring fees, and it'd be cheaper to charter a boat.

'I think we should sell it,' he told me. 'And the money we save on mooring fees we're going to treat ourselves to a month at the Colombe d'Or with.'

The Colombe is a small hotel at the entrance to the old town of St Paul with its shabby chic whitewashed plasterwork, scratched and scuffed. It's a haunt of the rich and famous, and particularly significant for the artwork on its walls, which initially came about when artists of the day left some work in lieu of payment – they're now worth a fortune. It's a very simple setting, with simple but well-appointed rooms and a pool, with the most amazing dining terrace covered in white parasols. Roger and Kristina loved it.

Part of its appeal is that it is quite exclusive and tourists popping in for a look are firmly discouraged, and if you don't have a lunch reservation don't even think of turning up on the off chance either. To my knowledge the menu has rarely changed in years, and is an oversized, handwritten (or painted) booklet. The first time I went there with Roger and Kristina they suggested we start with the basket of crudités – a huge wicker basket full with celery, spring onions, radishes, hard-boiled eggs, endives, cucumber … accompanied by a series of dips and sides, including sun-dried tomatoes, rollmop herrings, lentils, couscous, and various other things which I've no idea quite what they were – aside from being delicious. That was just the starter! My favourite main was the roast chicken and chipolata sausages – with a French twist. All served from silver platters, on their own unique crockery. Heaven.

The Colombe doesn't have many rooms, so they're sought after – particularly at the height of summer. The idea was to escape the heat of Monaco in August, that Roger and Kristina would decamp to the cooler mountain air, entertain or be entertained at dinner and lunch and, if need be, they could pop home in less than an hour to take care of any appointments or business. For the next eight years, this became their annual holiday. Many friends visited, and stayed, including Jeremy Lloyd, Joan Collins, Michael Winner, Leslie Bricusse, Elton John, David Beckham … and others.

Roger had been dining at the Colombe since the 1970s, and was quite often joined by Michael Caine, Sean Connery, Donald Sutherland, Robert Wagner, and once told me he saw Donald Pleasance sitting on his own, so thinking he was doing the friendly thing, Roger asked the maître d' to enquire if Mr Pleasance would like to join him and his guests.

'No, thank you,' was his reply!

The Colombe wasn't their only holiday destination by the way. On 14 April 2007, Roger and Kristina departed for Paris and three days later embarked on a road trip through the Loire Valley with their friends Michael and Shakira Caine, and Leslie and Evie Bricusse. Roger drove whilst Leslie and Michael took it in turns to navigate between the chateaux they'd booked. Lots of delicious dinners were matched by the most brilliant local wines, Roger and Kristina's favourite being a young Sancerre. They favoured the whites, especially light, crisp, dry ones, to avoid Kristina's adverse response to reds.

Roger's consumption was obviously moderate as he was driving, and aside from his expert shepherding of the gang he also devised the most perfect way of fitting the dozen cases they travelled with into the boot of the people carrier. When the others tried loading, they were always left with at least two suitcases that just wouldn't fit and waited for Roger to arrive!

I can only imagine the look on tourists' and fellow residents' faces when they saw the rather posh camper van pulling up outside and its A-list passengers pouring out.

A few years later, on the back of a UNICEF trip to Dublin, Kristina suggested it might be fun to spend a few days driving around Ireland and enjoying local hospitality – albeit just she and him this time. On 4 August 2010 they departed Dublin – in their friend Rita Crosbie's car, which she'd loaned them for the week – and spent two nights at Monart Spa in Enniscorthy, a night in Dunbrody House, Wexford, and then a couple of nights at Marfield House in Gorey before returning to Dublin. At lunchtimes they liked to stop at pubs and 'take a pint of the black stuff' as Roger called it. They were never short of conversation nor good company, and greatly enjoyed blending in with the locals and ambling around.

Meanwhile, Roger had spoken to the harbour master at Cap D'Ail, where he kept the boat, about selling it. It was suggested all that could be taken care of, for a commission of about 25 per cent. Though they added, 'It's not worth what you are asking.' That prompted Roger to ask me to sell it.

He actually wanted a very fair €60,000 – it was serviced regularly and very well looked after. I sensed some added value in the fact it was his boat, and it would be foolish not to take advantage of that.

'Don't go the traditional route,' I suggested to him. 'We'll sell it on eBay.'

'Ebay?!' he asked quizzically.

I'd recently read someone had sold a submarine on the auction website, so why not a boat? Roger took a few photos and sent me the 'blurb'. I listed it – as being owned by Roger Moore – and set the price at €60,000. Within hours a few queries came in from interested parties. One chap asked if it could be lifted for him to fly down and inspect the hull – I said sure, 'if you pay the harbourmaster for doing it'. The chap duly booked a flight, had it lifted and agreed the purchase price; a bank transfer was arranged and within a week Roger had the money in his hand. He gave it back to Kristina actually, saying as she bought the boat it was only fair she should have the money – she in turn told me she would instead buy him a new Mercedes for Christmas with it. In fact, I think it was one of the first Merc hybrid models.

Six or seven years later, we were in Bath at a book signing and the very same chap who purchased the boat appeared in the queue. He lived in Bristol and brought some photos to show Roger how it was being lovingly cared for.

I do like a story with a happy ending.

Roger's 80th birthday was looming and UNICEF got in touch with me to say they believed he was going to be in New York – on their behalf – on the special day, and they wanted to mark it. Being a charity they cannot of course pay for parties or dinners, nor would Roger want them to, but the New York office said one of their biggest benefactors was a great fan of Roger's and had offered to pay for a small dinner party (for twenty or so) to not only celebrate his birthday but to also say thank you for the sterling work he'd done and continued to do for the organisation.

'Who should be on the guest list?' they asked.

This called for a bit of subterfuge on my part, as I obviously needed to speak to Kristina about it and ask who she thought ought to be invited.

There were a few key UNICEF personnel, including the recently retired Mary Cahill who had been our main contact in the celebrity division for years (and with whom I always stayed in NY), Ann Veneman (Executive Director), Roger's dearest friend Aly Aziz … and Kristina also said, 'You.' Not that I'd been fishing, but I was delighted naturally.

Roger and Kristina were ensconced in New York before I left London and I made some lame excuse to Roger about not being in the office the next day as I had some dental work due. I had the idea of contacting the Prime Minister Gordon Brown, mentioning it was Roger's 80th; I never honestly expected a reply but knew he was a fan of Roger's. Soon after landing in New York I received a call, to say a letter was ready to be faxed – where did I want it sent? It was indeed from the prime minister and was a very personal, and very humbling letter.

Actually, when I landed at Newark I was called forward in the queue at immigration to have my passport stamped and fingerprints taken, along with the usual third degree, 'What is the purpose of your visit, etc.?'

'A birthday party,' I replied in all honesty.

'A what?'

'A birthday party,' I repeated.

'You've flown from London for a birthday party?' the officer questioned. I started feeling guilty – of what I'm not sure, but I started feeling it anyhow.

'Yes, for my boss.'

'He must be some boss if you're flying out here. Why isn't he having it in London?' he asked.

'Well, sir,' I replied, 'he is here working with UNICEF and it's his 80th birthday tomorrow – and they're throwing a party.'

'Oh yeah?' he asked.

'Yeah,' I gulped.

'So who is this boss of yours?' he continued.

'Erm. Roger Moore. The actor, you know, James Bond.'

'Roger Moore! Oh wow, I love him,' the official melted. 'Is he as nice off screen as he is on?'

And with that I was waved into the USA and almost given a police escort through the arrivals hall.

The dinner party, by the way, was held at Swedish restaurant Aquavit. Roger thought it was just to be him and Kristina having dinner, so imagine his surprise when he saw us all.

'You wanker,' he said as he hugged me.

There were many messages of congratulations from UNICEF offices all over the world, which were hugely touching.

'What shall we call it?' Roger asked, referring to the book once we'd returned home.

'Do we need to worry about that so early on?'

'I'd like to call it something,' he said, 'rather than *the book*.'

We kicked around ideas and thoughts. I told him it was important to mention Bond in there somehow, as that would be a major selling point, but Roger was always careful not to upset Eon, so was wary of it being too specifically James Bond 007. Eventually we hit upon 'My Word is My Bond'.

'I like that. Ask Michael O'Mara what he thinks.'

Word came back from our publisher that they liked it too. Of course, Roger spoke with Barbara Broccoli and raised the subject of including some photos.

'Roger – whatever you want is not a problem,' she told him. 'Whatever you want!'

I started by sketching out a structure – a chapter breakdown – and thought his film and TV work would be a useful backbone to the chronology, and chances are Roger would remember more things and details if we talked specifically about films and locations than he would just by dates. Unfortunately, he never kept any diaries, and aside from some paperwork on file with times, places and names of productions, there wasn't a lot of material to draw from. Roger never kept any of his scripts, schedules or call sheets; like with many other actors, they weren't viewed as being important or of any value, and simply took up room. If only he'd kept his scribbled-on scripts he could have sold them for an absolute fortune.

Once I had the structure and timeline, I said we should spend a week or so together to chat. We agreed just ahead of Christmas, when they moved to Switzerland, would be quieter with less in the diary and time to think. So I booked a flight to Geneva.

On arriving at the chalet in Crans-Montana, Roger said I was to freshen up and be ready to go out at 7.00 p.m. for dinner. Roger and Kristina had a number of restaurants they enjoyed visiting and depending on what they were in the mood for it would range from a fish place, to a chicken shack, to a pizza parlour or a little cafe out on the lake. Though when we were working, Roger preferred to eat lunch at home and quite often cooked cod, with a side of chopped boiled egg, horseradish and beetroot – Kristina assured me it was a Swedish speciality – it was actually very tasty, and we felt all the healthier for our wholesome lunches. Otherwise it would be maybe ham sandwiches, a cold collation of meats and cheese or something from the delicatessen. Roger always enjoyed a break mid-afternoon, and after a choc ice and coffee, would suggest we watch a movie. I think it was as much for him to take a sly nap as it was to give me a break.

In the mornings Kristina prepared their breakfast tray and took it upstairs – his one guilty pleasure in Switzerland was breakfast in bed – whilst leaving the table laid for me with juice, cereal, butter, jam and bread for toasting. Roger usually appeared soon after 9.00 a.m., having checked his email, made a few phone calls and prepared a few notes – he kept a notepad next to the bed as he often woke up in the night having thought of something for the book. He'd walk into the 'snug' where his big screen TV and DVD collection was housed, to find me waiting.

'Morning wanker,' was his usual friendly greeting, 'so where are we up to?'

Roger had asked if we could skip his early childhood and pick up from when he left school. I asked why, and he told me it was simply because he found thinking about his parents and those formative days as being massively nostalgic, happy and comforting. He said he'd woken up several times smiling, as he'd been dreaming about them.

'I'd like to type those pages myself, and then pass them to you,' he said.

He was enjoying the time on his own, thinking about his folks, and the more he was allowed to do it, the more they seemed to be with him. Roger wasn't a nostalgic sort of person, and I think always avoided memories that might upset him, but this was work, and so he allowed himself to relive those times. Though when I touched on his mother's death he claimed he honestly couldn't remember the year, let alone the date, as he'd blanked it from his mind.

We spent a good week chatting, making notes and reliving memories. I suggested we should maybe watch some of his films – he raised an eyebrow. He didn't particularly like watching himself on screen if he could avoid it, and when a film or TV popped up with him in, he'd talk about everyone else in it, the director, the producer, the locations, etc., rather than have to watch his own performance. Though I soon discovered he had an amazing memory for every film and TV episode he made, so didn't need to relive it. In fact, if I mentioned one actor from a film he worked on, he'd then tell me the episode, year and plot of a *Saint* episode they made together. His memory for faces and names was quite incredible, as it was for dialogue. He'd quite often tell me about audition pieces, including for his entrance exam at the Royal Academy of Dramatic Art (RADA), and would then deliver them word for word.

'I haven't heard that in sixty-five years,' he'd nonchalantly say.

I recorded hour upon hour of material, which I was secretly dreading having to transcribe as that's such a time-consuming laborious exercise, but all the same necessary.

'How long before you have it all for me to read?' Roger asked casually.

'Erm. Well …' I hesitated, buying some thought time, 'I'd like to think two to three weeks.'

Louise Dixon, our editor, was also keen to get hold of some pages as soon as possible – to start work as well as getting a flavour for the book's style (and no doubt to reassure Michael he hadn't wasted his money buying it!).

I duly returned back to base and in between manning the office, fielding enquiries, dealing with fan mail and anything else that came my way, I started typing.

Roger was a little nervous at this point – he'd always exuded confidence, but now he was laying his life bare, he was somewhat worried it might not be of interest. I kept assuring him it was, but the 'insecure actor' in him emerged for one of only a handful of times in my experience of working with him, and made him question himself.

After a week or so, I emailed him the first couple of chapters. A few hours later he phoned me up. He always started off by being positive.

'It reads very well. You've done a good job here,' then he'd pause for a couple of seconds. 'Now I've made some notes if we can run through it together?'

I could see why actors loved working with him as a director. He would never once pick on anything and turn it into a negative, rather he'd say, 'I think we can improve on what I said here.' It gave me confidence – as the more he questioned himself, the more I doubted myself too – and those Skype calls going back and forth were truly joyous. He'd also occasionally say, 'I think I was a little ungracious there, so let's rewrite that,' ever mindful of not upsetting any colleagues or co-stars.

The publishers were keen that Roger spoke about his earlier marriages, though he was adamant he didn't want to.

'You were obviously happily married – for most of the time together?' I queried.

'Hmmmm.'

'There must have been fun times, funny things, happy stories?' I continued.

'Hmmmm.'

'So I think to gloss over those, simply because the marriages ended in divorce, would be like glossing over your children.'

'What do you mean?' he asked.

'Will you chat about your children?'

'Of course I will,' he said.

'So why not your wives in the same positive tone?'

'You know,' he told me, 'I've always been married. From a teenager onwards I've never not been married or with a partner.'

'So marriage is important to your life?' I asked.

'Of course it is!'

'Let's talk about some of the funny stories. Let's talk about how you met. Let's talk about how those experiences made you who you are today. But let's not linger on the unhappy times or the break-ups,' I suggested.

Roger had always been the total gentleman and had never discussed his marriage breakdowns publicly for fear of upsetting the other parties.

'Just because I've been married four times doesn't make me a good husband,' he said, 'but I have learned, and I'm blissfully happy today with Kristina.'

'Would you have changed anything?' I asked.

'No, not at all.'

He did tell me he married Doorn van Steyn when he was 19 (and she was 24) because, although they were obviously in love, she had told Roger she was pregnant. She already had a young son, Shaun, and obviously saw Roger as a good father for the boy but it transpired she was not pregnant at all. Roger never said anything negative about Doorn, nor did he suggest she had 'trapped him into marriage', but there was obviously a niggling feeling at the back of his mind that he'd married young because he 'had to'. Had the romance taken a more leisurely course maybe their love would have been all the stronger for it, and the marriage lasted longer? Who is to know? But Roger asked we didn't mention anything about this, as Doorn was still alive and he didn't think it fair to spoil her life. He kept in touch with Shaun all throughout his life, so had reports from him about Doorn, and when the book was published Shaun wrote to tell Roger that Doorn had very much enjoyed reading it. Roger was happy about that.

Though one thing we did disagree on was the way he wanted to write about *Aspects of Love* – the Andrew Lloyd Webber stage show, which Roger was due to star in from April 1989. Roger simply wanted to repeat his reason for pulling out because he felt uneasy with the technical side of singing and hitting the right notes; he said he'd been having nightmares about it.

'Why don't you tell the real story?' I asked.

'I don't want to upset anyone,' Roger replied.

Roger had earlier told me how hugely excited he'd been about the opportunity of starring in a West End musical. He said it all started when he appeared on the *Dame Edna Experience* chat show and ended up in a song and dance routine with former Chancellor of the Exchequer, Denis Healey. Apparently, Lloyd Webber saw it, and thought Roger could make a good 'George' in the show – and a head-line name to sell tickets.

Roger engaged renowned singing coach Ian Adam, and with co-star Michael Ball and director Trevor Nunn, commenced rehearsals. Keen to show he could do more than just look brave as 007 on screen, Roger threw himself into the project wholeheartedly and was genu-inely so very happy.

Of course, Roger had always said he couldn't work if there was tension on a set (or stage) and so liked to keep the mood light, with a laugh and a joke here and there, which apparently didn't go down well in certain quarters. There was also a tabloid story suggesting Roger was having an affair (with Kristina) which may, or may not, have had a bearing. With his final rehearsals behind him, Roger flew home to Switzerland for the weekend, where he received a phone call saying it wasn't going ahead with him.

Roger fell into an armchair, totally shocked and stunned.

He was offered the chance to put out a press release saying he'd decided to pull out, which is exactly what he did and he stuck to the same line ever after.

'Would it be fair to say you were pushed?' I asked Roger. He didn't answer, just smiled and shrugged his shoulders.

CHAPTER 11

PUBLICATION

I spent another week in Switzerland, and lots of time on Skype, continuing work on the book. Though on my second trip out that year I developed a toothache at the front of my mouth and managed to ward off the worst of the pain with some over-the-counter painkillers. But one morning I woke and couldn't see much out of the tiny slits where my eyes once were – my whole head had swollen hugely and the pain was unlike anything I'd ever felt before.

I went downstairs, slumped into an armchair and couldn't really move. Minutes later Roger appeared and before he could hurl his usual abuse, looked at me and asked what had happened. I explained about the toothache, and he immediately got on the phone to his doctor and dentist; the doctor said she'd defer to the dentist, but it sounded like an abscess. I hated dentists. Or should I say, I was terrified of dentists.

'I'll be okay,' I mumbled.

Roger showed nothing but concern for me and could see the idea was obviously worrying me.

'I'll come with you and I'll sit with you,' he said quietly. 'There'll be nothing to worry about.'

To be honest, the pain was becoming so unbearable I'd have probably willingly agreed to see a butcher.

Of course, the dentist was thrilled to see Roger, and ushered me into a chair whilst talking in French to Roger. He looked into my mouth, whilst still chatting away to Roger, said something to his nurse who in turn handed him what looked like a huge needle – which he obviously pushed into my gum (I never felt it) as an explosion of pus followed by a massive relief of pain followed.

'You okay now?' he asked in English. 'You need to see your dentist when you get home, but it'll be fine. Roger says you're writing a book ...?'

We all chatted for three or four minutes and from that day on, I've never feared dentists again – though admittedly I don't get excited by the prospect of a visit either.

Within four months of starting work, we almost had a first draft. I think our contracted word count was 80,000–90,000 but Roger was keen to end with a chapter on UNICEF and he thought the best way of approaching it was 'around the world with UNICEF', talking about his trips, the purpose and some of the results. But it was clear this was going to take us well beyond the word count. Roger phoned Michael O'Mara to explain, knowing any more words would mean more pages, and that means more expense – and when the cover price has already been set, it means that expense comes out of the publisher's share of profits.

'We'll make more pages,' was the feedback. In fact, when Michael read the UNICEF chapter he also agreed to donate 20p from each copy sold to UNICEF. Roger's enthusiasm and passion was as infectious as ever.

Throughout the book Roger was keen not to offend and would always say to me, 'If you can't say anything nice, then say nothing at all.'

His silence about some people was deafening: Ray Danton, Grace Jones and Jean-Claude Van Damme being just three. However, when it came to David Niven, and his second wife Hjördis Genberg, a former Swedish model, to whom Niven had been married for thirty-five years, the vitriol and willingness Roger expressed to discuss 'the cunt', as he referred to her, was marked.

David Niven meant to Roger what, in fact, Roger meant to me – they were the closest friends, and Niv had been Roger's hero growing up. Roger would literally do anything for him and was so very proud to have shared the screen on a few occasions with Niv. But when David Niven became ill with motor neurone disease, his wife showed little sympathy – the marriage by this time was reportedly unhappy – and little care towards her husband. I had never seen Roger so angry and so hateful of anyone before, but when he saw his friend's life slowly ebbing away, and Hjördis too drunk to even care most days, he really did wish her dead in Niv's place.

David Niven was, like Roger, loved universally. At his memorial service the biggest wreath was from the porters at London's Heathrow airport, with a card that read:

'To the finest gentleman who ever walked through these halls. He made a porter feel like a king.'

That says it all.

By the time we wrote the book, Hjördis had long died and so the publishers didn't worry about being sued by her. By the way, Roger had sued several times in his life – once to stop the 'tell all' book Dorothy Squires threatened was about to be published, and many newspapers (mainly the *Daily Mail*) for printing malicious or simply untrue stories. He won pretty decent damages and, in fact, a couple of years before he died, had sued the *Mail* (twice) and the *Mirror* in the same year and, rather mischievously, asked me to keep an eye out for any other stories as 'Christmas is coming, we could do with a few more payouts.'

Ironically, Roger bought the *Mail* (and *Telegraph*) most days. He liked the *Mail* for the features, and the *Telegraph* for the crossword which he tried – but occasionally failed – to complete daily.

Lucy Fleming, niece of Bond creator Ian Fleming, contacted me to ask if Roger might consider being part of the centenary celebration of her uncle which was to take place at the London Palladium on Sunday, 5 October 2008.

Needless to say, Roger agreed wholeheartedly.

The curtain was raised at 7:30 p.m. on the night, to the infamous James Bond theme played by a sixty-piece orchestra followed by Lucy Fleming introducing the hosts of the evening, Stephen Fry and former Bond girl Joanna Lumley.

To the left of centre stage Jeremy Irons read passages as Fleming himself, and to the right former Bond villain Toby Stephens played 007 reading extracts from the literary adventures. A large screen displayed stills of Fleming, artwork, posters, and scenes from the films.

The most significant part of the evening was that Roger met Daniel Craig. Daniel and he shared a dressing room where they posed for a photo and Daniel thanked him for all his kind words of support. It was the only time the pair ever met.

Roger was joined on stage by eight Bond girls: Eunice Gayson, Maryam D'Abo, Madeleine Smith, Zena Marshall, Shirley Eaton, Tania Mallett, Caroline Munro and Joanna Lumley as a Sean Connery lookalike was quickly bundled off the stage by a Royale Marine Commando who abseiled from the roof. Roger gave a touching speech about Albert R. Broccoli, who saw the potential in Fleming's books, and then introduced the current producers Barbara Broccoli and Michael G. Wilson, who in turn treated the audience to a scene from the new film *Quantum of Solace* before Daniel Craig came on stage to rapturous applause to read the eulogy from Fleming's funeral.

Roger knew, as with films, that it's all very well writing a book, but you also need to enthusiastically embrace the promotion and marketing. Long before the book went to print, a marketing campaign was being put together with Ana Sampson at the publishers. With the book selling all around the world, requests were coming in from America, Australia, New Zealand, Hong Kong, Germany, Finland, Norway, France and other countries, all requesting that Roger visited, took part in press, and book signings. First, however, was a summer reception on 24 July organised by the publishers at Brown's hotel in Mayfair – a chance for Roger to glad-hand all the important book buyers for the big chains and distributors and, essentially, enthuse them into placing strong orders. Roger was an old hand at working a room, and I have to say he did it admirably, taking pointers from Ana all the time as to who was who, where they bought for and if they'd yet placed an order.

On the same day, I'd arranged for the manager of the Odeon Leicester Square, Chris Hilton, to meet with Roger and take his handprints for the walk of fame around Leicester Square. Chris had been at the Odeon for many years and hosted many premieres – including most of the Bonds – and during their chat, Chris asked if we'd planned a book launch.

'There are lots of signings going on,' Roger replied, 'but I'm not sure we've thought about a launch as such.'

'Would you like it at the Odeon? You can have the first-floor foyer and I'll happily lay on the catering – if you supply the champagne,' Chris suggested. It was an opportunity too good to pass up, and so I put a call through to Justin Llewelyn (son of Desmond) who was Tattinger's representative in the UK.

'You know you told me to ask if there's anything you could ever do?'

'Yes, Gareth. Just ask!'

'Could you supply champagne for 150 people at Roger's book launch?' I cheekily asked.

Without hesitation, Justin said, 'Sure. When and where?'

Roger took a very practical approach, a businesslike approach, to the book and its promotion. He asked which territories would benefit from him visiting – and that equated to 'what's the print run and how much advance have they paid?' Of course, some small countries had modest expectations, and that was reflected in their print run – if they were only printing 5,000 copies Roger wouldn't think it worthwhile visiting because any hotel and flight expense would wipe out all the profits, so what's the point? But in America they were looking to print 100,000 copies (on first run) which of course is a very different proposition. Hong Kong was viable as it was a stopover point en route to Australia and New Zealand, of course. It looked like Roger and Kristina would be on the road for two months towards the end of 2008, and another month in early 2009 when the likes of Sweden, France, Finland, Norway and Germany had had time to translate and print. It was a massive undertaking, but one Roger was keen to undertake.

Meanwhile our editor Louise was hard at work on our manuscript, and I was searching for photos and getting the necessary permissions to use them in the book.

If you think the point where you hand in the typescript is the end of the process, you're wrong – it's really the beginning of it. From the first editor coming back for review, it's then a case of pulling all the relevant photos together for captioning, and when all that comes back from the designer for (second) review, it's a case of carefully re-reading to spot errors, mistakes, omissions and so on. Turnaround time is fairly tight at each stage too, so you have to be on hand ready to dive straight in. In short, you live, breathe and sleep the book to the point of knowing it backwards.

When it does arrive from the printer, and you get your hands on one of the first copies, it's a very special feeling – almost like welcoming a child into the world. What you've worked so very hard to create, and with so many other people lending their talents too, has finally become a reality. Of course, some of those early copies are reserved for reviewers – particularly of the long lead-time magazines – and finally it's out there. How will it be received? Nobody really ever knows. But Roger reminded me of what he said on the way to the premiere of his first Bond film: 'It's coming, ready or not, and there's nothing you can do to stop it!'

Fortunately, the initial reception was positive and warm from fans and critics alike. The UK tour was fairly London-centric, as to be honest, the media he would be taking part in was all pretty London-centric, except for the BBC Breakfast news programme which is based in Manchester, but for which they agreed a rare pre-record in London with Roger. We did venture as far as Norwich, however, for him to sign a couple of thousand books at a wholesalers and a signing at Waterstones in the city; and similarly down to the south coast just outside Brighton to sign for another major wholesaler. The book tour lasted between 8 and 27 October 2008, kicked off with the all-important first interview, on the *Jonathan Ross Show* (then on BBC1); a book signing in Oxford; an interview and signing at the Cheltenham Literary Festival; signings at Waterstones in Piccadilly and Bluewater; interviews with just about every newspaper and magazine supplement; Radio 2 and Radio 4 interviews; *The One Show*; *The Paul O'Grady Show*; *The Alan Titchmarsh Show*; Sky Arts; *Channel 5 News*; local radio interviews and an interview/Q&A event at the National Theatre – a platform event, as they were called. It was literally non-stop for almost three weeks and we estimated Roger signed around 10,000 books at shops and for wholesalers/distributors.

'A signed book is a sold book; they can't send them back,' Michael O'Mara told Roger and consequently, at any shops we visited (or

passed through at airports), Roger took to signing any copies he saw
on the shelves.

The various book signings that were organised in shops were run
like military operations and limited to around 300 – people were
given a ticket to join the queue and once 300 were handed out, then
the queue was closed. Roger hadn't really met this many fans on a
one-to-one basis before, so was a little wary at first but soon got into
the swing of chatting and signing and posing for quick photos. The
secret was to keep the queue moving, and the person behind was
obviously keen to get in front of Roger so it generally worked well.
There was the occasional person who brought photos and memorabilia to be signed – having been asked repeatedly not to – and they
failed to comprehend that if he signed something extra for one, he'd
have to do it for others and, being on a sixty-minute or ninety-minute
schedule, that ultimately meant people in the queue with books might
not get it signed. Unfortunately, some of these 'fans' simply wouldn't
listen, and accused me and store staff of being difficult, claiming 'he
wants to sign it' as though they knew Roger and his wishes better than
we did. He liked to get in and then out as fast as possible.

You couldn't reason with these 'fans' – Herberts, as Roger called
them – and they were usually out to sell it on eBay, and would then
try their luck in the car park or at the loading bay, sometimes getting
very pushy and aggressive. Roger kept moving and apologetically said,
'Sorry we're in a rush', though they'd keep coming at him, and ultimately I'd turn and give a sharp 'Piss off' to them.

'I wish I could say that sometimes,' Roger later said in the car, 'but
I'm too nice.'

He'd occasionally nudge me on future outings and say, 'Give them
your greeting.'

You could usually tell the dealers and eBay crows as they never
wanted a dedication, only his signature and preferably with '007'
underneath.

'You get more for this do you?' Roger sometimes asked them as he signed one. They always looked surprised and shocked at the insinuation, before peeling back that particular photo to reveal another for signing. Roger just laughed and handed back their pen – they'd had one, so he'd been nice.

Towards the end of the tour, the initial sales figures were in and the charts were published:

Independent on Sunday – no. 6 in hardbacks, 26 October 2008
Review (Observer) – no. 8 in hardbacks, 26 October 2008
Seven (Sunday Telegraph) – no. 9 non-fiction hardback, 26 October 2008
Culture, Sunday Times – no. 8 bestseller, 26 October 2008

We were in the top ten of all the major newspaper bestseller lists. Roger was thrilled! I was pretty chuffed too.

Me with Desmond (Q) Llewelyn and *Carry On*'s Jack Douglas at the Theatr Clwyd 'British Film Weekend' in February 1993.

British Film Day, 9 April 1994 at Pinewood Studios. Gathered around the James Bond Aston Martin Vantage L–R are Burt Kwouk, Julian Glover, Valerie Leon, myself and Walter Gotell (my future landlord) (Photo: Robin Harbour)

The letter from Zygi Kamasa which led to us both setting up office at Pinewood in 1994.

My first photo with Roger, at Desmond Llewelyn's memorial event. (Photo: Joël Villy)

With Richard Kiel, in the Pinewood bar, getting one of his 'head smashes'.

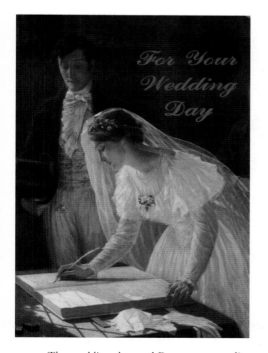

Christmas 2002

Dear Gareth,
We wish you a Merry Merry Christmas and a wonderful New Year.
And thank you for all your work and all the help during the year.
Much love Roger + Kristina

Zambia nov. 2002

My first Christmas card from Roger and Kristina.

SHERATON
PARK TOWER
London

Guest Stationery

Dear Gareth —
Merry Christmas!

THE LUXURY COLLECTION
Starwood Hotels & Resorts

101 Knightsbridge, London SW1X 7RN. Tel: 020 7235 8050 Fax: 020 7235 8231 Toll Free Reservations 0800 353535

A personal note to accompany a little Christmas gift.

For Your Wedding Day

FOR WHEN YOU TIE THE KNOT WITH LOVELY ALICE

Congratulations
on your special day
and
Best Wishes for the future
F...ING GOOD LUCK

THIS IS A DOWNPAYMENT FOR A NEW WIG.

The wedding day card Roger sent, sending me up about his stepmother Alice.

At Roger and Kristina's favourite restaurant, the Colombe d'Or in St Paul de Vence.
Clockwise: Roger, Deborah Moore, Andy Boyle, me, Kristina.

Lunch out on the boat, in Villefranche harbour.

Me reading out the congratulatory message from Prime Minister Gordon Brown at Roger's 80th birthday dinner in New York. (UNICEF's Executive Director Ann Veneman in shot with Roger and Kristina). (Photo: Lee Pfeiffer)

Us both with Pudsey, supporting Children in Need. (Photo: Tony Harwood)

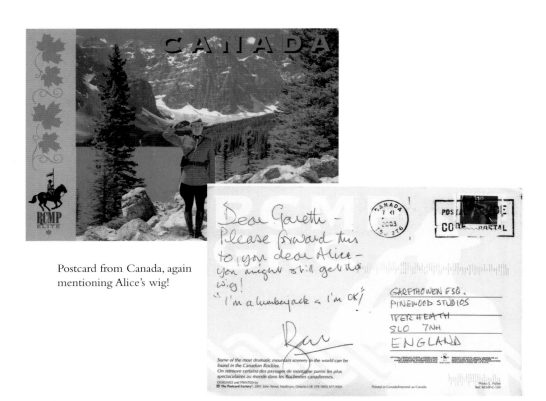

Postcard from Canada, again mentioning Alice's wig!

Dear Gareth –
Please forward this
to your dear Alice –
you might still get the
wig!
"I'm a lumberjack & I'm OK!"

Ro...

GARETH OWEN FSO.
PINEWOOD STUDIOS
IVER HEATH
SLO 7NH
ENGLAND

From left clockwise: Jerry Pam (Roger's long-time publicist), me, Damian Fox (animation director), Roger, Kristina, Andrew Chambers (Roger's FBI friend) and Joel Coler (publicist) in the port in Fontvielle at Le Michelangelo.

The book what we wrote. (Photo: Tony Harwood)

A Princess for Christmas, clearly showing Roger's bandaged foot after the hairy-arsed Bulgarians fell on him.

On stage at Pinewood at a Bond fan event, with me trying to interview Roger and director John Glen. Roger liked to try and support fan gatherings when possible. (Photo: Mark Mawston)

For Your Eyes Only, cast and crew united ahead of the screening at Pinewood. (Photo: Mark Mawston)

Andrew Freeman and me in Monaco for my birthday lunch with Kristina and Roger.

I found myself in Monaco on my 40th birthday, as you do. Andrew Freeman and Andrew Boyle joined us for lunch.

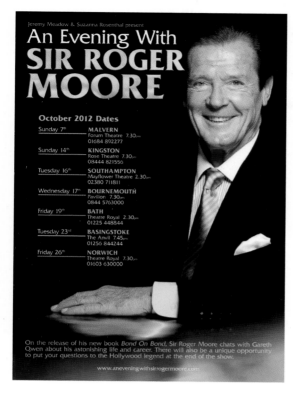

Our first tour in 2012.

Lady Moore photo bombing! (Photo: Stewart Crowther)

A sneak peek from the wings. (Photo: Stewart Crowther)

Sound test – usually consisted of Roger reciting dirty rhymes. (Photo: Stewart Crowther)

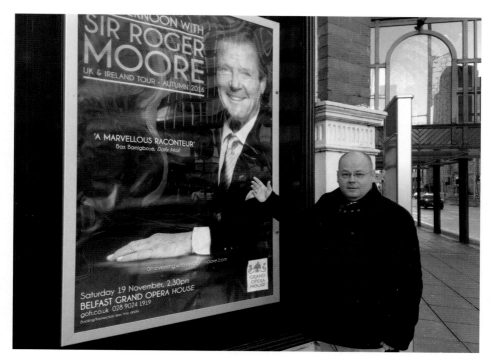

It pays to advertise! On tour in Belfast in 2016. (Photo: Stewart Crowther)

Backstage in Norwich. (Photo: Tony Harwood)

Producers Jeremy Meadow
and Suzanna Rosenthal
(standing) and tour manager
Mike Chalmers (kneeling
– as he always did in front
of Roger). (Photo: Stewart
Crowther)

A well-worn traveller, he has all he needs in his survival bag: pork pie, peppermints and the good
pub guide. (Photo: Stewart Crowther)

The tour team. L-R: me, Stewart Crowther (our so-called driver), Andrew Freeman (travel master), Steve Hill (technical supremo), Suzanna Rosenthal (producer – hence two hats), Mike Chalmers (tour manager), Lesley Pollinger (book agent), Aron Mills (work experience).

Much the same crowd, just different venue!

The tour bus. (Photo: Stewart Crowther)

Signing his fan mail one day, Roger said, 'Here — words of advice for you!' and handed me this photo.

Roger sketched this, in Hamburg.

THE CELEBRATION OF A LIFE

Sir Roger George Moore, KBE
14 October 1927 – 23 May 2017

Saturday, 10th June 2017 at 11 o'clock
Saint Paul's Church, Monte-Carlo

10 June 2017 — my birthday, and the day of Roger's funeral.

The Stage. (Photo: Mark Mawston)

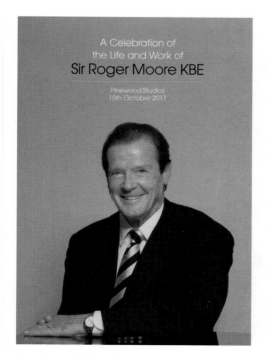

The Memorial Brochure.

One of the invitations I designed, with a little help from Dave Worrall.

Roger's final resting place in Monaco.

I once dreamed of my own office at Pinewood. That dream, and a whole lot more, really did come true.

Roger and Kristina look over me in the office, in a lovely painting by Gary Morgan.

CHAPTER 12

THE BOOK TOUR

Following the UK tour, I joined Roger and Kristina on a PR trip to New York where Collins books kept him just as busy as the British publishers had. Although hard work, it was really enjoyable and memorable, not least because Roger took me to some of his favourite restaurants in the 21 Club, Cipriani on Central Park – where he introduced me to Buzz Aldrin and a peach Bellini (where it was created), the St Regis (where the Bloody Mary was created – though I declined) and others in between press and signings.

Although we were obviously expected and on the guest list for the various TV shows, in post-9/11 New York we were asked for ID on arrival at the various studios. Our very efficient publisher/publicist usually stepped straight in with my and his driving licence and said, 'This is Roger Moore – he is expected,' and Roger was waved straight through. Well, on all but a couple of occasions; the first was when a rather officious front desk guy at NBC made a point of showing he was totally unimpressed with everyone and anyone.

'I need his ID,' he grunted and nodded towards Roger.

Roger stepped forward with his Monaco residency card.

'No good,' grunted our new friend.

'What do you need?' Roger asked.

'Proof of who you are!' he snapped.

'It's my country ID card,' Roger reasoned.

'Not acceptable,' came the next grunt.

The TV show staff had meanwhile appeared and tried to tell the desk guy that this was the special guest, but he wasn't having any of it. So Roger, full of charm and with a smile, put his autobiography onto the desk. 'There's my photo on the front of the book, and there's my name – is that good enough?'

He was waved through.

Also on the show were two American actors, Paul Rudd and Seann William Scott, who had a new film out. Rudd was quite well known (even more so now!) and Scott was famous for playing 'Stifler' in the *American Pie* films. They sidled up to Roger in the wings.

'Hey man, you're Roger Moore. James Bond.'

'Yes. Hello, how are you?' Roger asked. 'What are you here promoting?'

'We've this new movie called *Role Models*. But we grew up with you as Bond. Wow, this is so great to meet you.'

'Why thank you, I'm pleased to meet you two too – I hope the movie is a big success,' and with that Roger was called onto set for his interview. When he came off set and saw the crowds of girls outside calling for the acting duo, he was suitably impressed. 'Famous, are they?' he asked me.

'Yes,' I replied.

'I'm fucked if I know them …' he nonchalantly said as he walked with me to his dressing room.

Our final TV interview was with BBC America. Our publicist couldn't join us but said it was all set up and the BBC representative would be waiting in the lobby to welcome us and whisk us through.

However it never happened that way, as on arrival at their studio building, an ex-traffic warden who had been elevated beyond his capabilities to front desk security, and who had let his new-found power go to his head, stared at us blankly.

'Hello, I'm Roger Moore and I'm here for a BBC ...'

'Passport!' was the curt reply, as he held his hand out.

'I'm sorry I don't have my passport with me. I'm expected though and if you'd call up to ...'

The ex-traffic warden interrupted, 'I've said I need your passport!'

'I don't usually walk around New York City carrying a passport. I'm here for an interview with BBC America. If you'd kindly call through to them they'll come down to meet me.'

'Nope,' was the even curter reply.

'Well fuck you then,' Roger snapped, and told me to follow him to the car. Just then the BBC journalist appeared and came dashing after us.

'I'm so sorry, Sir Roger.'

'Am I not expected?' Roger asked.

'Yes, but security is all a bit over the top, I'm afraid,' came the apologetic reply.

'If I'm expected somewhere and spend an hour crossing downtown to get here, I do not appreciate being snapped at by a rude, arrogant desk clerk who didn't even have the decency to call upstairs.'

'Yes, but as I say security has gone a bit over the top,' he laughed.

'I've been in New York for ten days, travelling between TV and radio studios, and I have never been treated so rudely – and this is the BBC! My home TV station!' Roger replied. 'If you don't have the staff with good enough manners to treat guests with courtesy when they arrive, whoever they are, then I've no wish to be interviewed by you.'

He got into the car. 'Driver, would you kindly take us back to our hotel?'

'But Sir Roger ... you're expected on the nightly news ...' said the BBC man.

'I suggest you put that idiot security guy on in my place then,' Roger concluded, and closed the door.

'What wankers,' Roger said to me. 'Now, will you join us for a nice dinner as it's our last night in town?'

That was the only time I'd known Roger to walk out on an interview – not that he'd walked in – but he couldn't ever bear rudeness, not least when it was directed his way.

Roger and Kristina then went on to Hong Kong, Australia and New Zealand. I didn't accompany them, as for one thing it was hugely expensive, but I also had some family matters to take care of back home. However, I rejoined them for press trips to Paris (cue more lovely restaurants), Oslo, Amsterdam and Helsinki – where our publisher proudly boasted, 'You are booked into the city's second-best hotel.'

'What's wrong with the best hotel?' Roger asked mischievously.

Oh, and then there was Germany. I think this was the nearest I'd seen Roger to really losing his temper.

He and Kristina had been travelling for many weeks and had to carry all sorts of clothes – including evening suit and dress – and consequently I'd made it very, very clear to the various publishers that they'd need a people carrier type vehicle (especially when I was with them too) on arrival at the airports, as there were around six suitcases and a couple of carry-on type bags. It had all worked very well until we landed in Hamburg. Firstly, someone had obviously tipped off the Herberts that we were coming as a huge gang, with loads of Bond photos, were waiting in the arrivals hall along with photographers. The publisher's representative was also waiting, revelling in the attention his author was receiving, and seemed somewhat surprised that we had two trolleys of luggage as he led us to his car – a four-seat saloon BMW.

'Is this it?' I asked, in disbelief.

'Yes,' he said proudly, 'BMW have given it to us for free.'

I could see Roger's face tense up, but as the gang of Herberts were still following and pestering, I suggested he and Kristina get in and we'd see what we could do with the luggage. We actually ended up squeezing three quarters of it into the boot and the rest on the front seat, and I crawled in between Roger and Kristina on the back seat, holding a bag on my lap.

'Did you not get the memo about all our bags?' I asked him.

'Well, the car is free,' he repeated.

Roger asked if he worked for the publisher or was a driver by trade.

'I do everything,' he said, just as he clipped a wing mirror on a parked car.

'Please concentrate on the road,' Roger urged him.

As we pulled around to the Atlantic Hotel there must have been thirty or forty photographers and Herberts standing outside the front door.

'Keep driving,' I instructed. 'Is there a back way in?'

'Why?' he asked.

'Do you really need to ask? We're buried in luggage, look like we've been dragged through a hedge backwards and you've arranged a press call on the steps!'

'It is well known you are staying here,' he replied.

'Only because you've told everyone,' I snapped back.

There was, thankfully, a loading bay around the back of the building where we could pull in and prise ourselves out of the car. But as soon as we entered the lobby, the mass from outside came piling inside. It was the most unorganised, stressful arrival ever.

We finally managed to get into a lift and up to the suite, which turned out to be the most inhospitable, dark, sparse room I've ever seen. The so-called sitting room consisted of two dining chairs plonked in the centre of the large room with a small coffee table in front. Walking through to the bedroom, we saw a double bed and dressing table.

'When was this room last used?' Roger asked.

'It's a great view,' the idiot answered, before telling us we were running late and the conference started in ten minutes.

'What conference?' Roger asked.

'We have a photographer and all the store buyers here.'

I asked where my room was, and conveniently it was two floors below and on the other side of the building.

Ever the pro, Roger said he'd freshen up though Kristina was understandably not at all happy, but even so suggested he went to the meeting and she'd unpack and sort things out.

A dining room on the ground floor was pointed out to us by the idiot, and we entered to find about twelve people sitting down, in total silence. Roger cheerily greeted them and asked the idiot if we might have some drinks as he clearly hadn't thought to offer anyone one. The awkward silence of the gathered crowd continued and the idiot made no attempt at introductions – he just stood there smiling from ear to ear.

'I know,' said Roger, 'why don't we go around the room so everyone can introduce themselves?'

That at least broke the ice.

A painful twenty minutes later, having posed for selfies and signed autographs, we managed to make our excuses to leave for dinner. Roger usually invited the publisher to join us for a meal, had they not already taken the initiative of organising one for us, but in this instance he hadn't, and Roger didn't.

He simply asked the idiot, 'What time do we start tomorrow?' as a means of dismissing him.

'10.00 a.m.,' was the reply.

Over dinner, Roger said that the publisher was sure to send a PR representative the next day and we'd be saved from the idiot. Alas, that was not to be! The idiot turned up and duly escorted us up one floor to the 'James Bond Suite' where he excitedly told us Pierce Brosnan had filmed in *Tomorrow Never Dies*. The room was beautifully furnished, bright, welcoming and tasteful.

'If this is the James Bond suite, why aren't I staying in here?' Roger asked in all seriousness.

The idiot didn't have an answer.

'Is it booked out?' Roger continued, in his line of enquiry.

'No, we have it.'

'So what's the problem? Why are we in that horrible room downstairs when this is here – empty?'

'We have booked it for interviews,' was the reply, 'to impress journalists.'

'How about impressing your author?' Roger questioned.

It was agreed that they'd switch rooms, which the hotel was actually delighted with as it was good publicity for them to say they'd had three 007s in there – a few years earlier I'd been there with George Lazenby for MGM publicity.

Every territory has their own way of working, I realise, but when we were told bookshops fully expected Roger to sign any memorabilia fans brought in, alongside books, I really did question why. Surely a publisher organises signings to sell books? The more people they get through the queue, the more books they sell. Yet here they were more worried about fans going away happy because they'd had memorabilia signed, and they fully expected Roger to remain until he'd got through the entire queue. I told Roger that whenever he felt he'd had enough, we'd call it time.

It took about twenty minutes to get through the first six people in the queue, who'd all brought five or six things each to be signed plus the book. I told the publisher this was just plain crazy, but rather than see it from his author's point of view (and sales team, no doubt), he just shrugged. Roger said he'd sign one item only with a book, as that was the only way the queue would get through, but even after nearly two hours there was still a crowd who hadn't had their books signed, and Roger apologised but said, 'If they hadn't made me sign everything else I could have done it, but I'm tired, my arm is aching and I'm afraid they've scheduled interviews so I must go now.'

On the way back to the hotel, Roger asked that I phone Lesley (our literary agent) and he told her we'd be leaving for home the next day, as the publisher had an idiot running things. Lesley made some calls, and our idiot appeared suitably chastised and apologetic later that afternoon; he promised there wouldn't be any more signings of anything but books. Roger agreed to stay, and the next day we were set to travel to Berlin before then going on to Cologne.

Whether someone was watching the hotel, or had knowledge of our schedule, I'm not sure, but when we arrived at the railway station there was a gang of Herberts waiting for us; similarly at the other end in Berlin. They were the most aggressive, nasty people and really spoiled the trip.

Our German sojourn was the last in the *My Word is My Bond* publicity schedule, and whether we were slightly jaded I'm not sure, but it was without doubt the toughest, most badly organised experience of all. As we parted ways to fly home, Roger hugged me tightly and said, 'Thank you for your help here – I really mean that.'

CHAPTER 13

PORK PIES & THE POST OFFICE

In all my years with Roger I never pried into his affairs. If he told me something, then fair enough, but I never asked him anything he didn't volunteer. Whenever he called me, I knew if he started off by saying, 'Hi Gareth, how are you?' it was to be straight to 'business' – sure enough he'd follow up with a pressing request for something, or to book tickets for flights, reserve a hotel, or maybe write a letter, and so on. If he said they needed to go to Geneva for a couple of days, for example, I'd never ask what for – that was none of my business – I'd just make the arrangements.

Conversely, whenever his calls started with, 'Hello Mister Owen,' or 'This is Sir Roger Moore here, international star of stage and screen ...' I knew they were going to be more chatty, less pressing calls. One day, in the wake of the financial crash of 2008, which affected pretty much everyone in one way or another, Roger called full of fury so naturally I *had* to ask what the problem was. He rarely ever discussed personal finance matters with me, but was seemingly very angry and very worried, with expletives flying right, left and centre, along with his accountant's name.

He explained that his accountant, in the weeks after the crash, had done nothing to react or to minimise his (Roger's) investment portfolio's exposure, and consequently he'd lost what he termed 'a lot of money'. Roger was not only angry that his trusted financial advisor had taken his eye off the ball but, worst of all, seemed rather casual about it by saying, 'things will pick up'.

Roger had always planned carefully and whilst it hadn't exactly plunged him into dire straits, it did mean he'd have to tighten his belt as he wouldn't have the anticipated income from investments and savings he'd been so diligent to arrange for his old age. It certainly meant he couldn't afford to retire any time soon.

'You know, people used to say to me we don't like him [the accountant], but I never listened, did I?' he pondered.

I'd never experienced Roger so angry, though it went beyond money. It was a matter of trust and faith – and if Roger had a fault it was that he tried to like and trust everyone. Most of the time his judgement was spot on, but only occasionally wrong.

The accountant was dismissed and Roger never forgave him nor spoke to his so-called friend of over thirty years ever again. Many months later the accountant wrote to me, suggesting I tell Roger that he only ever had his best interests at heart – I filed it.

Janus Friis was incredibly kind at Christmas 2008 and presented Roger and Kristina with details of a holiday he'd booked for them the following February. He reasoned Roger had worked so hard on the book tour (and knew he'd been very unhappy with other events) that they deserved to get away from it all in the Seychelles. He'd booked two weeks at Soneva Fushi just them, a sea villa and good food and wine.

Whenever he was asked, 'What's your favourite destination?' Roger always answered, 'Home!' – he'd been pretty much everywhere and had grown fed up of airports and all that was entailed in getting through them, so I could tell he was a little unsure about accepting the holiday. It was a long flight, and the idea of a 'beach holiday' never appealed to Roger, but Kristina told him it would be ideal to totally relax and unwind, and he *needed* to do just that.

A couple of days after leaving for the trip, Roger phoned me from his beach villa.

'It's just us and the ocean. Bloody marvellous. So relaxing. And the food! Oh my god, it's fantastic. Wish you were with us ...'

'I could fly down,' I offered.

'Sorry, the phone line is fading in and out, I never caught that, anyhow have a nice sandwich for lunch, won't you? Bye!'

Talk about rubbing my nose in it. Though he often did; in fact once he mailed me the whole menu from a restaurant having carefully ticked off what they'd ordered and wrote, 'We thought of you as we were stuffing our faces.'

A few months later, in May 2009, I visited Roger in the South of France during the Cannes Film Festival, which I started attending in 1995, and he presented me with a huge box of chocolate biscuits; he and Kristina had just returned from a UNICEF trip to Lithuania, where the head of the Vilnius committee apparently asked Roger to thank me for helping with the trip arrangements and to pass on the gift.

'I've carried these all the fucking way for you,' Roger smiled, 'and I've resisted opening them.'

It would have been a hassle for Roger to pack them in his luggage, so I was particularly touched he'd done that for me.

He was often presented with gifts on trips, though it sometimes proved a bit of a nightmare in transporting them – especially paintings and heavy books where we'd have to arrange a courier. Sometimes the best meaning of people presented the most awful gifts – the sort when you receive them for Christmas you feign appreciation but secretly wish they hadn't – but Roger genuinely was grateful and though it cost him more in transport than the item was probably worth, he always made sure nothing was left behind. If flowers were presented, he'd take them back to his hotel and then suggest to the UNICEF representative, or to me if I was with him, to ensure they went to someone who would like them, but to take them out via a back door so the sender didn't see and think he was rude. As Roger might only be in a hotel for a night or two, the flowers always outlived his stay and he thought it a terrible waste.

Quite often when doing TV shows in London there'd be flowers and a goodie bag – including things like a luxury pen, cologne, diary, books, etc. – in his dressing room, and Roger would say, 'Would you like to take these flowers for your mother?'

I'd tease him by saying, 'Thank you – I like pens myself.' He wouldn't react, but would simply slip it into his inside jacket pocket, and say, 'There's a few biscuits left on the plate over there you can have.' He was the first to admit he loved anything for free. 'I'm such a ponce,' he'd boast, 'especially if it's worth a few quid.'

Though I once made the error of telling the producer of the Paul O'Grady chat show that Roger loved pork pies and so they presented him, live on air, with a huge platter of them from Fortnum's and Harrods. Roger took a slice and thanked them – though they boxed the rest up and sent them down to our car.

'I daren't eat any more of these,' he said as we reached the hotel. 'Would you take them?'

Half of my corridor at Pinewood feasted on the very best, and most expensive, pies the next day.

Roger once said something about pork crackling and loving it on a Sunday roast, and a company got in touch to say they manufactured pork scratching and asked if he'd like some – I said sure. A huge great big box arrived at Pinewood, and later that day when Roger came into the office he looked at them, then looked me squarely in the eye and said, 'I like Rolls Royce cars, Aston Martins and big houses too!'

However, such was Roger's visual enthusiasm and delight on Paul's show, that whenever he returned there were piles of pork pies awaiting him in the dressing room, and other shows followed suit. What was a casual remark about enjoying a pork pie with a dollop of tomato ketchup became a trademark rider – or so productions thought.

Forever after, at book signings, stage doors and charity events, fans would press a wrapped pie into his hand as though they were delivering him a chunk of gold; though he always followed the advice of Terry Wogan and said, 'Never eat food you're sent in the post or given on the street.' I think bitter experience taught him that lesson!

In May 2009, the British Film Institute were marking the centenary of Cubby Broccoli's birth with a season of his films and talks with some of his colleagues. Barbara Broccoli asked Roger if he would consider participating in an evening event, being interviewed on stage by David Walliams.

'Anything for Cubby,' was his reply.

He and Kristina then departed for their month at the Colombe D'or in the South of France, and towards the end of their sojourn Roger phoned me with the news that he'd been offered a commercial for the Post Office; it was to shoot in September, paid well, but that was all he knew at that moment. A few weeks later he phoned, rather excited, to let me know they were going to shoot it at Pinewood. 'Isn't that great!' he exclaimed.

The morning of the shoot, I arrived in the office extra early and around 7.30 a.m. Roger phoned to say he'd arrived but there was no one to meet him, no one around F-Stage where he was dropped off, and he wondered what was happening. I dashed over to find him chatting with the director, who Roger had sought out in the depths of the set – they apparently hadn't expected him so early, yet it was their car that had picked him up. Roger was escorted to a huge trailer and said, 'Come on, you can keep me company.'

It must have been an hour or more before anyone appeared, and that was to take Roger over to the make-up lady, who put so much powder on Roger's face that he looked very pale and quite ill. Another hour or so went by, until an assistant director popped his head into the trailer asking, 'Are you ready, Sir?'

We walked onto the set, and Roger made a point of introducing himself to everyone, when the director said, 'Shall we go for a take?'

'Aren't we going to run through it all first?' he asked.

'Why?' countered the director.

'I'd like to see the lighting, where you're shooting from and what tracking we have …'

'Oh. I see,' replied the rather perplexed director. 'Well, we are a bit pushed for time,' he added, looking at his wristwatch.

I could sense Roger becoming annoyed but he kept his cool and said, 'Humour me two minutes would you?'

They walked through, and Roger asked if the other actors could take their positions as he'd wanted to 'get their eye lines' but the director seemed increasingly impatient.

'He has been here hours,' I chipped in, 'so it's not as though he's making you wait.'

Of course, all the other actors were grateful for a run-through, as you never quite know what to expect when you work with someone for the first time. It was a comedic commercial, and of course timing is everything with comedy and Roger wanted to ensure he had the right beats in his delivery.

After a few set-ups, they called lunch and asked Roger what he'd like from the canteen.

'I'm going for lunch with Gareth in the restaurant,' he replied.

We walked over to the Pinewood restaurant and had just finished a main course before an assistant appeared to say they were ready.

'Forty-five minutes for lunch?' Roger asked, realising he'd have to forego a much-loved post-lunch espresso coffee.

We walked back to the stage to find the director looking at his watch, but again Roger remained calm and composed. He took a quick look at his lines and said, 'I'm ready when you are.'

The final shot came around about 5.00 p.m. Roger was to take a bouquet of flowers from a female Post Office staff member, mouth the words 'Thank you' (as there was to be a voice-over at that point in the ad) and walk off camera. After about five takes, where the director kept saying 'slower', 'a bit faster', 'slower again', Roger – feeling a bit peeved at the indecisiveness – mouthed a very clear 'Fuck off' on the next take.

'Sorry! Didn't get that one,' called the director from his seat at the side of the set. 'It didn't look like "Thank you" to me.'

It was lost on the director!

Back in the trailer about 6.00 p.m., I asked when Roger's car would be with us.

'We have some B-roll stuff to shoot first,' the assistant said.

'B-roll?' I quizzed.

'Yes, a little Q&A in the trailer and a few behind the scenes shots,' he added.

'But why didn't you do that earlier when he was twiddling his thumbs in here?' I asked.

'It's okay Gareth, how long will it take?' Roger chipped in.

'No more than an hour,' came the reply.

'Hang on. He's been here since 7.30 a.m., he's tired, hungry and needs a drink I wouldn't wonder, and you seriously expect him to do another hour? Is B-roll even in his contract?' I asked.

'Let's just do it,' Roger offered. 'The quicker we do, the sooner I'll get home.'

Roger was too soft for his own good at times, but like a true pro he did everything they asked, and even signed autographs and posed for selfies.

'Ask for me on the next commercial,' he called out as he got into his car, 'and I'll speak to you in the morning,' he added as he looked at me. 'Now go home.'

When the commercial finally aired Roger felt he 'looked like death warmed up', and a cameraman from some of his Bond films phoned me up demanding to know who had lit the set, saying, 'They've made him look terrible.'

Still, the fee eased Roger's annoyance!

Robert S. (Bob) Baker had been Roger's producing partner on *The Saint* from the early 1960s, and post-*Saint* they made a movie called *Crossplot* together in 1969. They were also neighbours for many years in Stanmore, north London, and Bob was even godfather to Christian Moore.

Their friendship extended beyond business though they remained partners in subsequent years in their production company TRI Ltd. They often chatted over the phone and occasionally got together, plus of course worked as executives on the 1996 movie reboot of *The Saint*. Bob also became a good friend to me when I took over from Doris Spriggs, and in fact Doris and I lunched with him a couple of times a year and really enjoyed his company. In the late spring of 2009 Bob phoned me to say he'd spoken to Roger and wanted to let me know too that he had been diagnosed with cancer. He said he wasn't going to subject himself to treatment that might give him an extra few months or a year, and at 93 felt he'd had 'a good innings'. He seemed remarkably calm and at ease; a great light in Bob's life had already gone out, having lost his dear wife Alma six years earlier. Bob explained there was much to do, and that – with Roger's agreement – he was going to appoint his daughter Marilyn as a director of the company to ensure a smooth transition.

We spoke a few times subsequently and even met for lunch, but I knew the inevitable was only a matter of months. On 30 September, Bob succumbed to his illness. Roger was dumbstruck.

Without doubt Bob had been responsible for building Roger as a star in *The Saint* and *The Persuaders!* and they of course led to even greater fame as 007. Roger took his death very hard.

In accordance with his faith, Bob's funeral was to be a day later. Roger asked me to book a flight for him to the UK, but it proved impossible to get him to London in time for the service.

'Do you think we could do something special for Bob, like you did for Peter Hunt?' he asked. A few years earlier, at the behest of former Bond editor and director Peter Hunt's friends, I organised – on Roger's behalf – a celebration gathering one Sunday afternoon at Pinewood. It was a chance for friends and colleagues to come together, raise a glass and remember Peter with some speeches, film clips and conversation. Roger picked up the bill.

I left it a few days before speaking to Marilyn, but then mentioned Roger's wish to hold an event in celebration of her father. She became very tearful and said, 'He'd have loved that.'

We set plans into motion for the following April.

Towards the end of 2008, Roger and Kristina flew back to London for a UNICEF/British Airways event, before then flying to Dublin for a UNICEF fundraiser. The Dublin committee asked if Roger would give a talk about his career for half an hour, as part of the fundraising dinner, but he said he always felt awkward about standing up and 'rambling on' about himself, and instead suggested I accompany him and do a little interview/chat on stage instead.

Of course, I was delighted, and we had great fun – so much so, Roger kept it at the back of his mind for when he was asked to tour UK theatres in 2012; but that's another story, a little later.

CHAPTER 14

SAINTLY ENDEAVOURS

Everything was coming together remarkably well for Bob's celebration. It was to be held in the magnificent ballroom at Pinewood – where in fact Bob had filmed many times – and would celebrate every aspect of his life and career, from his important work as a cameraman during the Second World War, for the Army Film Unit, through becoming a director and producer to being a much loved father and grandfather.

Many friends, colleagues and actors had signalled their intention to attend, including Ian Ogilvy, flying in from LA, who had followed in Roger's footsteps as Simon Templar; Francis Matthews, Derren Nesbitt, Carol Gardner, Britt Ekland, Victor Spinetti, Burt Kwouk, Valerie Leon, Madeline Smith … and many others.

It was to take place on 18 April and Roger was flying in the day before. Only he couldn't.

On 14 April, a volcanic eruption in Iceland slowly closed on European airspace; two days later, on 16 April, it was announced flights from the South of France would be grounded. Roger asked that I look into rail connections to Paris from Monaco, as Charles De Gaulle airport was still operating flights, but no sooner had I done so than news reached us of Parisian airports closing too. The Eurostar, naturally, became booked up very quickly and I asked Roger if he wanted me to get a couple of the last seats on the regular train up to Paris, where I could drive over (via a ferry service) and meet them.

'But the roads around Calais will be chaos,' he cautioned, having seen pictures on the news of mad dashes to ferries by stranded holidaymakers in Europe. Even as he was saying it, trains were showing up as 'sold out' as well as the ferry operators.

Ian Ogilvy arrived at LA airport to be turned away too. He emailed to say, 'There's no way I can get out of the US.'

It was a calamity.

'Do we cancel?' I asked Roger.

'People have made arrangements. The family is expecting. How many others are flying in?'

'Just you and Ian,' I replied.

'Then the show must go on. Is there a way I can link up?' he asked.

We had a big screen and projector coming in, so I suggested I could look into a Skype connection for Roger to appear on the big screen.

That's exactly what we did, and although Roger wasn't there in person to welcome everyone, he could at least share some time with us, and reminisce a bit about Bob. It was a very poignant day.

The volcanic ash incident also impacted on other arrangements Roger had made in the UK, including addressing the Oxford Union. The university had invited Roger several times over the years, and this particular time it looked as though it could all work, and was scheduled for the Wednesday.

Sunday and Monday passed. On Tuesday there was talk of some airports reopening and flights resuming, so I made a few calls and got Roger switched onto the first flight out of Nice to London on the *fazed*

Wednesday morning – it was actually the first flight out of the airport, period. Roger and Kristina weren't <u>phased</u> by being amongst the first to fly through the now deemed 'safe' ash cloud; their attitude was, 'If the experts say it's fine, then it must be.' Though Roger did phone on touching down at Heathrow to say they'd made it, with a sigh of relief!

It was straight into a car and off to Oxford, picking me up en route.

Roger loved meeting enthusiastic youngsters and at the supper they'd arranged ahead of his little talk, Roger asked, 'Which of you here is going to be a future prime minister?'

Roger spoke about acting, Bond and then about UNICEF, which seemed to grip the students more than anything else. 'These are our future leaders and politicians,' Roger said to me. 'It's important they are aware of UNICEF and the pressing issues facing children, as they are the generation to solve it all.'

A few days later in central London, Roger gallantly stepped in for Sir Christopher Lee at the last minute to receive an award on his behalf. The Cinema Retro Magazine Lifetime Achievement Award was bestowed upon Sir Christopher, and he'd agreed to pick it up at a special 'audience with' event at County Hall. Earlier in the day, a huge number of Bond alumni including director Lewis Gilbert, actors Richard Kiel, Maud Adams, Britt Ekland, Jesper Christensen and others attended 'Fanfest' which was held in honour of the film series, featuring interviews, prop displays, meet and greets and so on. The late afternoon 'Audience With …' Sir Christopher was a ticketed event and the highlight of the day. But the day before, citing a slip in the bath, Sir Christopher's representative cancelled his appearance.

Not only would there be 200 very disappointed fans, there'd be an award left unpresented.

The publishers asked me if there was any way Roger might come along and pick it up, whilst reminiscing to the audience a little about his friend.

'Sure, if they send me a taxi from and to my hotel,' he agreed.

Roger dutifully attended, spoke for over half an hour and made a lot of people very happy.

Two days later, Roger attended a lunch at the Ivy which Richard Kiel had organised to discuss a film project. Sir Christopher was also there.

'How are you Christopher? Hope the fall wasn't too nasty?' Roger enquired.

'What fall?' the actor queried.

'I picked up an award for you on Saturday because they said you'd taken a fall.'

'Oh. Yes. Well, it wasn't really a fall …'

'A political fall?' Roger asked. 'To get you out of it?'

Sir Christopher shuffled awkwardly and changed the subject!

Roger was always honest when responding to invitations – when they were 'no thank you' it was always a swift and firm 'no thank you'. He'd never leave it hanging, nor allow people to think he was on schedule to attend if he had no intention of doing so. Not everyone shared his diligence, unfortunately.

Rounding out the trip, on 14 May, was a visit to Buckingham Palace where Roger and Kristina mingled with students from film schools, who were part of the Films Without Borders initiative. Launched by HRH Prince Edward, The Earl of Wessex along with *Star Wars* creator George Lucas, the non-political UK registered charity provides hands-on educational film-making workshops for youths between the ages of 15 and 19, and crosses all borders – an initiative Roger was keen to support.

The rest of the year involved trips to Sweden, Denmark, Germany, Spain, Austria, Switzerland, Croatia and France. Roger showed no sign of slowing down, and there was also a steady supply of scripts coming his way, from low-budget schlock horror to Bond rip-offs, gangster stories and (supposedly) high-budget drama – though the budget obviously never made it as far as hiring decent writers most of the time! There was probably one a month coming in, on top of the almost daily TV, radio, newspaper and magazine requests.

One particular film offer which grabbed Roger's attention was from a Spanish production outfit, who were offering $1 million for a couple of weeks' work, playing a guest lead.

'Would you read the script and tell me what you think?' Roger wrote in an email, attaching the screenplay.

Who wouldn't be interested for that amount of money?!

The first scene had Roger's character, a wheelchair-bound professor, having oral sex being performed on him. The next scene was with his character in an S&M sequence.

I didn't read beyond, but called Roger and told him.

'Don't bother reading any more,' he instructed. 'I'll tell Jean I'm not interested.'

'Shouldn't you look at it?' I asked. 'After all it's a big offer.'

'I wouldn't get beyond page one!' he exclaimed. 'Having a blow job on screen?! Please!'

He was very principled and also very conscious of his image as a UNICEF ambassador – money was always secondary. He probably turned down 99 per cent of what he was offered because he felt it either poor, badly written or a waste of his time.

Into the latter category fell a Christmas episode of BBC hit series *Sherlock*. It was all very hush-hush, and Jean Diamond was sworn not even to tell her secretary that there was an offer coming in for Roger to make a one-day guest appearance, let alone see a script. Of course, Roger's first question to her was, 'Where is the script?'

A bike was dispatched to Jean's office with the three pages from the scene (not a full script – no chance of that) and she had to sign a non-disclosure agreement before it could be left with her, and a second one assuring the producer Roger wouldn't divulge any information either. Since it transmitted some years back, I think I'm safe to talk about it now!

Roger phoned me, in a foul mood.

'How dare they!' he said. 'What a nerve!'

'What's happened?' I asked.

'The BBC want me to do *Sherlock*. They've sent the scene, on watermarked pages, to play an old fart in a club with one line. One line! I'm copying you in on my reply to Jean.'

With tongue firmly in cheek, and with reference to the line offered, he wrote:

Dear Jean,
I am doing a little rewrite on the scene...

THIS IS INTOLERABLE ... I HAVE BEEN WAITING FOR SOME TIME EXPECTING A SCRIPT AND YOU EXPECT ME TO GET OUT OF BED, MAKE A FIVE HOUR TREK TO LONDON ... TO SAY ONE FRIGGING LINE ... IT HAS NOTHING TO DO WITH PLOT OR EVEN CHALLENGING, EVEN FOR A FIRST YEAR RADA STUDENT ... STICK YOUR PUDDING UP YOUR BUM ... THANK YOU AND GOODNIGHT MRS CALABASH WHEREVER YOU MIGHT BE!

much love, Roger

Ouch! I think Jean was more diplomatic in her reply to them.

Though there was one little project Roger was more enthused with when Sky were contemplating another series of their *Little Crackers* Christmas specials – short films featuring famous names retelling an incident from their childhood – which was to centre around Roger's pet monkey when he was a child living in Stockwell and the mischief it created. The plan was for Deborah Moore to play his mother, whilst Roger would narrate and it was proposed the comedian Will Smith (*The Thick Of It*) would pen the script based on Roger's memoir.

But the broadcaster didn't go ahead with the second series, and so the idea was shelved.

CHAPTER 15

HAIRY-ARSED BULGARIAN ELECTRICIANS

The following year, 2011, started off relatively quietly, with him and Kristina binge-watching all the Oscar contenders on DVD at home in Switzerland. He'd receive upwards of 100 DVDs to consider each year, to then vote for 'Best Actor' – academy members tend only to vote in their field of expertise.

Then, on 31 January 2011, Roger was preparing one of his marvellous dinners of bollito misto for some friends who were due to visit that evening; the recipe involves cooking vegetables separately to various meats, all prepared at different times and temperatures and you have to bring them all together to a conclusion in a salsa verde, and there is therefore a lot of standing around involved. Roger's Swiss chalet kitchen has under-floor heating, so by the time the first guest arrived he felt absolutely exhausted and was sweating profusely; in fact he had to lean on a high stool as he literally couldn't stand up any longer.

Kristina insisted he went upstairs to bed and said not to worry about serving dinner as their friends would understand. She meanwhile called the local doctor as, in Roger's own words, he 'climbed the fifteen stairs through waves of nausea, and at the summit was violently sick in my bedroom'. The doctor duly administered an injection to stop the vomiting, settled him down and said he would come the next morning; when the doctor did return it was to take various blood samples and later in the day they called to say the results were in and he needed to go to hospital.

'When, tomorrow?' he asked.

'No Roger, you need to go now!'

A local friend drove him and Kristina to Sierre, where he told me, 'They left me to the tender mercy of a gentleman intent on inserting a catheter you-know-where, and through a haze of painkillers I remember there being an endless list of more tests and injections in swift succession.'

A doctor said he was sorry that the weather was so bad, because he wanted to call an air ambulance to take Roger to the hospital in Lucerne for surgery. Instead, he explained, Roger would have to travel in an ambulance by road. Despite heavy pain relief Roger complained of feeling 'every single bump on the drive'. On arriving at 3.00 a.m. he was wheeled straight into the operating theatre to be anaesthetised in the excellent University Hospital (CHUV). According to notes he kept, apart from blood pressure being 180/88 he was also suffering with a kidney stone blockage, and that was coupled with his pace-maker deciding it was overdue for a battery change; it all combined to make him feel rather ill and weak.

The surgeon set to work and placed a catheter internally to help the stone, after some planned ultrasonic a week or so later, pass more easily. He also fitted a new battery in his pacemaker and Roger recovered quite rapidly, feeling much better and with renewed energy. Happily he was discharged on 12 February 2011 to be home in time for their traditional romantic Valentine dinner.

A couple of weeks later he returned to hospital to 'hammer' the kidney stones with ultrasound shock waves, and the stent was left in place to help the stones pass.

Then came a call from American producer Brad Krevoy, which saw a call to action stations. Roger had worked for Brad a decade earlier in a film called *Boat Trip* (2002) and now Brad was putting a Christmas TV movie together for the Hallmark channel, and offered Roger a role in the family-friendly drama *Christmas At Castlebury Hall* (which later became *A Princess for Christmas*). Filming was to be in Bulgaria – where an attractive tax incentive was on offer, and where costs were a fraction of those in Western Europe and America – and Roger would be playing a duke – the head of a household – when a young American woman arrives, at the invitation of the duke, with her young adoptive charges who are in fact related to the duke. A love story blossoms between her (Katie McGrath) and the duke's son, Prince Ashton (Sam Heughan).

Roger liked the script, and asked Jean Diamond to 'do the deal' as he and Kristina prepared to fly. Roger's scenes were contained within one week of shooting, so I knew I wouldn't hear a great deal from him as he'd be busy with long days whilst I stayed in the Pinewood office keeping everything else ticking over. Though he did call briefly a couple of days into the shoot to say all was going well, but two days after that he called again to say all was not going so well – there'd been an accident on set. Roger had tripped over a cable on set and taken a tumble, and jumping to his aide 'three hairy-arsed Bulgarian electricians' actually fell on top of Roger – one across his groin – and pulled down a heavy lamp (attached to said cable) onto Roger's leg. The lamp pierced his shin plus the weight of it and the electrician combined to crush his lower leg. He was taken to the doctor who patched him up, whilst his ankle started swelling to epic proportions.

'They're saying I may need a skin graft, and I can't put any weight on my foot,' he told me. Though, ever the professional, he added, 'We only have one day of shooting and they think they can do a little re-write to have me sitting down – with my foot elevated, out of shot.'

Sure enough, and in great pain, Roger completed his scenes – much to the relief of his producer friend, who then arranged a private jet to take Roger and Kristina back home to Monaco.

Three days later Roger started developing a temperature that went up to 39.5, and that wasn't helped by his blood pressure being all over the place and him vomiting. The doctor came over and immediately whipped him off to the Princess Grace Hospital where they discovered the stent had been dislodged by the burly, hairy-arsed Romanian spark. He wasn't too happy at the thought of more surgery, but decided if it was necessary then he wanted to go back to CHUV in Switzerland and Professor Jichlinski. An air ambulance from Monaco to Geneva was arranged with onward road transportation to Lausanne. Time was of the essence as he was suffering from a kidney blockage and septicaemia was setting in.

The professor operated and replaced the internal catheter, and whilst Roger was recovering they took a look at the injury to his shin; the wound wasn't healing at all well, and they suggested it would require a skin graft. Enter another professor, this time Lee Ann Laurent-Applegate, from the Department of Musculoskeletal Medicine & Plastic and Reconstructive Surgery Regenerative Therapy Unit. Lee was absolutely brilliant and in fact a firm friendship was established that day. She took several samples of his skin and cells during the skin graft which were analysed, and later she asked if he would be willing for the pathology on his blood cells to be photographically enlarged and used in an exhibition explaining cellular regeneration, as he was deemed a prime specimen with miraculous cells! He liked that.

He was later asked if he'd do a voice-over for the exhibition, which has since travelled the world.

The skin graft healed well and despite suffering from a painful ankle for several months, he was able to start walking properly again, albeit wearing tennis shoes. He even attended a couple of formal functions resplendent in his blazer, trousers and white trainers!

In the midst of all this hospital attention, I attended the Cannes Film Festival in May of that year to see that *A Princess for Christmas* was on the screening schedule in the 'market' (films being offered for sale to overseas territories).

'But we only finished it a month or so ago,' Roger cautioned. 'It must be a different film.'

It was indeed his film – and aside from a couple of lines of dialogue re-recording and end titles being completed, it was pretty much the finished film.

'What did you think?' Roger asked.

'I really enjoyed it. It was good fun.'

He seemed hugely relieved – his bravery had proved worthwhile!

During Roger's convalescence in the summer I pitched an idea to him.

'You know next year marks the fiftieth anniversary of the Bond films?'

'Hmmmm?' he mused.

'Well, you also know you're one of the only Bonds who will talk happily about your years in the part, and you know full well we'll be inundated with interview requests?'

'Go on …' he said.

'So why not have something to talk about? Something to promote.'

'Such as what?' he queried.

'A book! I was thinking, a book on Bond, by Bond.'

'What, to talk about my seven?'

'No,' I explained, 'about the whole series, the whole world of 007.'

'I've not seen them all though,' he cautioned.

'You saw *Die Another Day,* and Daniel Craig's two – his third is out next year too. I have DVDs of the others.'

'But there are so many books on Bond out there, what can I say that's different?' he asked.

'Quite simply – you were Bond. That's the difference.'

He nodded a slight approval, though I could tell he was unconvinced. So I placed a call to our agent Lesley, who immediately said, 'Yes, yes, yes!' and phoned Michael O'Mara. The publisher said, 'Yes please!' and asked us to deliver in the late summer of the year for publication in 2012.

'I suppose we'd better do it then,' concluded Roger.

I suggested we map out what we thought the book should be – definitely photo-rich, insightful, funny, informative and accessible for Bond buffs and casual readers alike. We tossed around ideas of the format and decided to go for all the familiar elements: girls, cars, gadgets, locations, plus add in premieres and merchandise too.

As the months passed Roger's injuries improved and he was able to progress from wearing tennis to proper shoes and planned a trip to London. We'd had a couple of enquiries about some of his shows being released on Blu-Ray and if he'd be involved – in September *The Persuaders!* was going to launch and Network (on behalf of ITV) asked if Roger might attend a Q&A event.

They suggested Barry Norman – who Roger had known for years – would be the host interviewer, and it would be followed by a signing. They agreed to cover Roger and Kristina's airfare and hotel for a few nights, so that suited him nicely. It was actually a fun evening and the Aston Martin DBS from the show was on display outside the venue in Knightsbridge.

Being an advertised event, there were a number of Herberts hanging around outside. There were a couple of particularly unpleasant ones – a young boy and his 30-something mate who were not only pushy and threatening in manner, they followed us back to the hotel and ran into the lobby, blocking Roger from the elevator and demanding he sign photographs.

I was not happy. Okay, outside a venue he is fair game to ask for an autograph, but inside his hotel, his home, no way. I asked them to leave, but they started mouthing off that it was a public place and they were entitled to be there. Hotel security came over, but the 30-something claimed he was staying there (though declined to give a name or room number) and the younger one mouthed off to the security guys: 'I'm 15. You can't touch me. I'm a minor. Touch me and you're in trouble.'

I managed to usher Roger into the elevator whilst they argued with hotel security, and then asked the front desk to call the police who, in fairness, arrived within a couple of minutes. The hotel staff were obviously worried other guests would be alarmed or disturbed, but the Herberts were adamant they were not leaving the lobby. Just as the police arrived the older one ran out, into his car and disappeared but the younger one mouthed off to the police about him being a minor and they couldn't touch him.

I explained they'd been hassling us all evening, and the 15-year-old said: 'All I want is a photo signed for my grandmother and he [pointing at me] is being threatening and nasty.'

I could see hotel guests arriving back from their evening out were looking worried at the sight of policemen in the lobby.

'Look,' I said to one of the policemen, 'If I get this photo signed, will he go quietly and not come back?'

'Will you?' they asked the boy.

'Yeah sure,' he replied.

So as a compromise I said I'd pop upstairs with it. 'Who is it dedicated to?' I asked.

'Just signed,' was his reply.

'What is your grandmother's name?' I asked again.

'She doesn't want it dedicated,' he snapped.

'She? Or you?'

I shrugged at the policeman and said, 'Ebayer obviously', but took it upstairs – being sure to stop the lift on three different floors going up so they didn't know which one Roger was staying on.

Once I handed the photo over, the policeman said:

'You've got your photo. If I hear you've come back here – 15 or not – we'll take you for a nice trip in our car to the station.'

With that, he was off.

Roll forward a couple of years, I was at a book signing with Roger and saw this little lovely chap in the queue. I recognised him immediately. As he approached the front of the queue he noticed me, and turned his head away.

'I assume you're no longer 15 now?' I asked him.

'Eh?' he said, innocently.

'How's your grandmother – still collecting is she?'

His face went bright red and he grabbed his signed book and disappeared.

The second DVD project was *Sherlock Holmes in New York* – a film Roger made in the 1970s – being released on Blu-Ray for the first time, and they asked if Roger would maybe record a commentary.

'Why not,' said Roger, 'if they spring for a few nights of my hotel stay.'

He really enjoyed seeing the film and chatting about it and all the characters involved, which was all followed by a nice lunch at Quo Vardis in Dean Street.

Meanwhile, *A Princess for Christmas* was going to be released on DVD in the UK a short time after its broadcast on the Hallmark network. The UK distributor asked if Roger would undertake some publicity in the UK in the run-up to Christmas. As Roger and Kristina enjoyed coming to London for Christmas shopping, it seemed a perfect opportunity – and again they offered to pick up flight and hotel costs so it was effectively a free trip in exchange for half a day of his time.

Radio and TV shows were lined up, and a publicist – Alex – assigned to accompany and look after Roger as they moved from BBC radio, to ITV and others. At one point they were running a little ahead of schedule, around 11.30 a.m., and whilst driving near Piccadilly Roger noticed they were near the Wolseley restaurant.

'Can we stop, Alex? I wouldn't mind a smoked salmon bagel and scrambled egg as I had breakfast at 7.00 a.m.,' he requested.

'Sure, okay, we have time. I'll wait with the car,' Alex replied.

'No. You'll come and join me, my treat. C'mon,' Roger added.

That was typical of Roger – so kind and thoughtful.

The next day we received the following email:

Dear Gareth,

Just a quick note to say thank you to both yourself and Sir Roger for all your help and hard work with making yesterday possible.

It was a pleasure to meet and spend time with Sir Roger yesterday. He truly is a consummate professional and a wonderful man, to say the least. It was an honour for myself and all those with whom Sir Roger came into contact with just to be in his presence.

I say this without wanting to be too gushy but I can't actually help myself.

Wishing you a Merry Christmas, Happy New Year and once again, thank you both so much.

Best,
Alex

CHAPTER 16

BOND ON BOND

Along with me visiting Roger in Switzerland to record conversations for the book, Roger had enjoyed a quiet few weeks at home before, in February 2012, attending the Opera Ball in Vienna – a huge annual society event which takes place at the Vienna State Opera, dating back to 1935.

It was a particularly cold winter evening and he was wearing formal white tie and tails, without any overcoat. Traffic around the opera house was horrendous and so he told Kristina they should get out of the car and walk over, as otherwise they'd never get there on time. That sprint through the cold air resulted in him developing a cold which, by the time they got back to Switzerland, had developed into full-blown flu.

After a couple of days confined to bed, the doctor sent Roger for some X-rays on his lungs, and upon seeing the results she said, 'Hospital!' His heart sank at the thought of going to the CHUV in Lausanne and Kristina having to endure a ninety-minute drive each day to see him. Nothing worried him more than Kristina worrying about him.

Fortunately, after a couple of calls the doctor discovered there was a lung clinic in their hometown of Crans-Montana, and they were able to admit him. Various tests followed and he was diagnosed with double pneumonia – this being the second time in his life. As a child, he wasn't expected to live, and this time round it looked pretty bleak as he didn't initially respond to any of the antibiotics administered.

His body was weak and limp, his mind was just a haze and he was propped up in bed with tubes and drips attached. Anyone seeing him would have thought the end was nigh.

The doctors tried various combinations of medication until they hit upon the strain of antibiotic that seemed to have some effect. The dosage was huge, recovery was very slow and it really hit him hard, and cost him the use of his legs.

He was due to fly into London to record *Piers Morgan's Life Stories* but of course there was no way that was going to happen. I spoke to the producer and explained the situation, asking that the news be kept strictly confidential as the last thing we needed was a story in the press saying he was on his deathbed. They were terribly kind and supportive, even sending flowers, and said they'd happily reschedule just as soon as he was fit and well.

People started calling the office at Pinewood, worried he hadn't replied to emails and phone calls, but rather than explain he wasn't well, I found it easier just to ignore everything and not have to make excuses or tell lies. However, Barbara Broccoli detected something was wrong when Roger hadn't returned messages, and she spoke to me about him – and of course I had to fill her in.

Poor Kristina spent every day sitting with Roger, holding his hand and talking about anything and everything to try and perk up his spirits. She returned home and fell into bed every night, totally exhausted and mentally drained.

Fortunately, Roger started responding to the medication and once they removed the infection from his lungs – which wasn't very pretty – he was told he should be able to return home soon. Meanwhile he'd lost the use of his legs with the illness and had to learn to walk again with the aid of some wonderful physiotherapists. It wasn't easy but

Kristina always said he was a very good patient as he listened to his doctors and did as they said; plus she said he had a strange fascination with being in hospital, watching everything that was going on and taking a clinical interest in all the various treatments and medication – it's also why he enjoyed watching medical dramas on TV, only he was then starring in his own private episode.

One of the side-effects of the strong antibiotics was that his hair started falling out at a great rate. He told me he comforted himself in the knowledge that his friends Yul Brynner and Telly Savalas made successful livings as bald actors, so it wasn't all bad.

At least he hadn't lost his sense of humour!

Meanwhile, we'd been hard at work on the book *Bond On Bond*, as it became called, and I was able to pass my transcripts to Roger to read during his recovery and make notes with his comments and additions – it was coming together really well, and Eon productions had been incredibly helpful with granting us access to their photo archives. Barbara had said, 'Whatever Roger wants will not be a problem.'

Our literary agent called to see how Roger was feeling, and to chat about an idea. With the book coming out in October, Roger would undoubtedly be asked to do some book signings around the country, and asked how he might feel about doing some added value events such as Q&As. Roger said if it helped sell books, he'd be open to suggestions.

'How about "an afternoon or evening with" type events at a few select theatres, followed or preceded by a book signing?' she asked. She then explained she'd like me to meet a couple of theatre producers, Jeremy Meadow and Suzanna Rosenthal, who had experience of this type of production.

We all met for lunch and the plan was to 'try out' with six or seven theatres within reasonable distance of London, tying in with book signings, and as it would make Roger accessible to his fans on a significant scale for one of the first times ever, it should – they said – prove a popular ticket.

I relayed it all back to Roger who seemed enthusiastic and asked about the finances – would it be worthwhile, being the bottom line? Initial projections showed it would indeed be.

'I'd have to sit on stage and do a Q&A?' he asked.

'Sort of. The first half would see you chat about your career, and then in the second half you'd open it up to a Q&A towards the end,' I replied.

'Oh I can't sit on stage and talk. I'd go off at tangents and run over time. I need some sort of direction.'

'A script?' I asked.

'God, now you're scaring me to death. A script? I couldn't remember all that.'

'Well, how about you have someone on stage with you like Barry Norman did a few months ago at that *Persuaders!* launch?' I suggested.

'I like Barry … but I'd prefer you … you let me talk,' he added. 'Would you do it with me?'

I told Roger I'd love to, though suggested I should get a little compensation.

'Of course!' he said. 'How much?'

I suggested a modest share of what he got – a percentage. That way if it did well, I'd benefit, and if it flopped he wouldn't be out of pocket.

A little negotiation ensued, and we agreed a figure.

'I do so hate talking money,' he said.

'I'm cheaper than Barry Norman!' I quipped.

Jeremy and Suzanna confirmed theatres in Malvern, Kingston-Upon-Thames, Southampton, Bournemouth, Bath, Basingstoke and Norwich over a three-week period – into which would fall book publicity too. It would just be me and him on stage, in two armchairs, chatting.

Advance copies of *Bond On Bond* arrived from the printers and I remember being at Pinewood with the producer of *Piers Morgan's Life Stories* rearranging dates when Roger phoned me.

'It's just arrived! It's really, really beautiful. Such an elegant book. Well done. I think we're going to make a few quid on this!' he said excitedly.

Whilst he had seen and approved the proofs, there is something quite different in holding a completed book in your hands, something quite special and beautiful. After a period of ill health earlier in the year, Roger was now full of energy and enthusiasm for the work ahead!

From August onwards, Roger started the PR assault by undertaking a number of long-lead interviews with the likes of *Woman's Weekly*, *Daily Mail Weekend*, *GQ* magazine, etc., and then flying into London on 5 October ready for *The One Show* magazine programme on BBC1, before being driven to Cheltenham for the literary festival, where he took part in a short interview about the new book before departing for Malvern the next day for our first 'Evening With …'

I had previously asked if he wanted to rehearse, and he declined saying, 'I prefer spontaneity. I don't like to know what your next question will be.'

Of course, he also admitted he could be lazy when he wanted to be too!

Joining the team was our tour manager Mike Chalmers and Roger's regular driver Stewart Crowther who would chauffeur Roger and Kristina from place to place, sometimes with me joining them in the car, or quite often I'd travel separately from home to meet them at a venue.

In the weeks leading up to that first show I made some notes and knew I had to get from his childhood to *The Saint* in the first half and then to *Bond* and UNICEF in the second half, allowing fifteen minutes for questions at the end. Of course, with no set format/questions I could hop around a little if needed, or conversely linger a little longer too.

In the dressing room Roger appeared completely relaxed ahead of the first show, laughing and joking. I won't say I was nervous, but I was a little anxious. A thousand people in a packed auditorium can make anyone feel a little anxious.

I walked on stage, and the one benefit of having bright spotlights shine on you is you can't actually see anyone in the audience – you can rarely see beyond the front edge of the stage – so in a way, it felt as though it was just going to be him and me there.

I introduced him, and he walked on to a riotous applause. I honestly felt the floor shaking in the building. Roger beamed widely, and we took our seats.

We chatted for what seemed like five minutes, but a quick glance at my watch made me realise it had been almost an hour. I prompted Roger with questions, to tell the fun and juicy tales he'd told me time and time over, and Roger knew how to time a laugh and how to pace a story – he had the audience in the palm of his hand. We went to the interval and again he received an ovation; he floated offstage and to the dressing room, so very happy. He was even happier to see a pork pie and ginger ale laid out for him by Mike.

The second half started with *The Persuaders!* and Roger did a brilliant impersonation of Tony Curtis, before moving on to Bond – the audience collectively whimpered with excitement as he delivered his famous introduction – 'My name is Bond, James Bond' – before exploding with appreciation. To be in the same room as their favourite 007 was something most of the audience members had never dreamed possible, so you can appreciate just how excited they were – and they lapped up his stories of leading ladies, gadgets, cars, villains and his thoughts about Daniel Craig 'being the best Bond ever'. He was so modest.

When it came to the Q&A, there were the usual 'Who is your favourite Bond girl?', 'What's your favourite gadget?' (which Roger answered as though he'd never been asked before) to queries about working with David Niven, Richard Burton and Richard Harris. I think just about the only thing Roger and I discussed in advance was UNICEF – I suggested we leave it right to the end, and Kristina added, 'You should tell the Audrey poem.'

The poem was actually a letter, written by Sam Levinson to his granddaughter, which Audrey Hepburn had read to her children on her deathbed. It summed up her inspiration and passion for being such a passionate UNICEF ambassador, and it was Audrey who had introduced Roger to the organisation.

So the final question went to me: 'In the last twenty years or so, you've devoted yourself to UNICEF. Can you tell us a little about the charity and its work?'

Roger spoke so eloquently and so very passionately about things he'd witnessed, campaigns he'd helped raise awareness of, and how thousands of children around the world died every day, needlessly, from preventable causes. He then recited the Sam Levinson letter which ends with ...

'If you ever need a helping hand, you'll find you have one at the end of your arm; and as you grow older, you'll find you have two hands – one for helping yourself, the second for helping others ...'

The theatre fell silent. The audience was moved to tears – I'd defy anyone not to be.

Roger rose to his feet, thanked the audience and we left the stage.

'I think we got away with that,' he said in his dressing room and opened the awaiting bottle of champagne.

Our kindly producers had spoken to UNICEF ahead of the tour and asked if we might be able to have some donation buckets for the foyer, in the hope of raising a few hundred pounds. In fact, over the five years we toured we raised over £30,000 in loose change and the occasional note. Roger was quick to reassure audiences that every single penny went to helping children, and his revelation to them that $1 (80p) could actually save two children who were dying from dehydration made it all the more tangible.

Our next theatre gig wasn't for a week, and so in-between Roger returned to London and recorded a podcast for *Empire* magazine, an interview with Steve Wright on BBC Radio 2, a pre-recorded interview for BBC Breakfast, an appearance on *This Morning*, a book signing at Harrods, and then appeared on QVC.

We'd all heard about how bookshops were disappearing off the high streets, and there being fewer and fewer places to buy books, so when our publisher mooted QVC, Roger thought it was a bit of a joke. They wanted him to go on, twice, in the same day for half an hour and just chat about being Bond and his book. In return the channel guaranteed to buy thousands of signed books. (Roger signed book-plates, which could be stuck in the volumes, and had previously signed 5,000 front pages which were inserted into the books ahead of binding.) In that one day, Roger sold more books than he would in fifteen national bookshop signings.

He did continue with store signings at Waterstones Bluewater and HMV Oxford Street along with visits to distributors in Norwich, Bath and Eastbourne – not to mention after some of the theatre gigs. When there wasn't a signing at a theatre, Roger signed books in advance to be sold in the foyers – and they proved hugely popular too.

The release of the book tied in nicely with Daniel Craig's third Bond outing, *Skyfall* (2012), and Bondmania was everywhere. The premiere of the film was going to be held at the Royal Albert Hall and, of course, Roger received an invitation for 23 October – but we were going to be on stage that very night in Basingstoke. Roger really wanted to see the film, not least to continue singing Craig's praises, and so I asked Eon Productions if there was any way he could see it ahead of the schedule.

Their post-production period was running up to the wire – nothing new there; Roger always used to joke the titles were still wet on his Bond films when they premiered – and the only real chance would be on the Saturday morning, 20 October. That worked for us.

Eon arranged for the film to run at 10.00 a.m. at the Sony preview theatre in Golden Square.

'You'll come won't you?' Roger asked.

'Sure! Can I bring a couple of mates?' I enquired.

'I can't see why not, the more the merrier.'

Roger, Kristina and myself, along with Andy Boyle and Andrew Freeman, enjoyed our very own private screening of *Skyfall*. It was quite surreal sitting there, watching it with Roger.

We all emerged united in opinion – it really was a brilliant film. Roger felt assured he could continue raving about Daniel Craig as the best ever Bond. He also enjoyed telling audiences in Basingstoke that he'd seen the film and could guarantee them a fantastic night out when they went to their local cinemas.

Just as with *Skyfall*, the book and theatre tour was a great success with sold out audiences and queues wherever he went.

Eighty-five-year-old Roger had developed a new lease of life and relished every single minute of it.

Following the weeks in the UK, we then flew to New York for a week of activity there – interviews, TV and radio chat shows and a signing on Fifth Avenue at Barnes and Noble all followed.

One interview, with a glossy magazine, was carried out over lunch at his hotel – the St Regis – and he asked me to tag along. The journalist was very complimentary of the book, which was always a good start, and Roger invited him to order from the menu.

'Is there anything you recommend?' the journalist asked as he scanned the upscale fine dining choices, obviously feeling a little out of his comfort zone with white linen napkins and polished silver cutlery.

'Sure,' said Roger with a smile, 'I always have the hamburger.'

The journalist smiled and said, 'I'll join you.' Roger had a knack of putting people at ease.

They started chatting and our burgers arrived. Roger applied liberal amounts of ketchup onto his, and to the somewhat puzzled gaze of our new friend, picked up a knife and fork.

'You eat your hamburger with a knife and fork?' he asked.

'Doesn't everyone?' Roger countered with a trademark eyebrow raised.

It was a jolly half-hour interview after which Roger asked for the bill.

'No, this is mine,' said the journalist. 'I have to pay as I can't be seen to be influenced …'

'Nonsense!' Roger exclaimed. 'You're my guest and I'm paying. Feel free to write what you like, I won't be offended.'

It was a hectic but good week in New York, with lots of US-wide publicity bagged.

On returning to London, Roger agreed to guesthost the BBC's comedy news quiz *Have I Got News for You*. He always enjoyed watching it and thought it'd be a nice easy gig, reading from autocue.

How wrong he was.

The writing team came to meet him on the day before recording, to run through gags, check what Roger was happy with, and to chat about any thoughts and ideas he had to contribute. The next morning soon after 9.00 a.m., he was picked up for the studio and rehearsals – the constantly evolving and changing script (with lawyers on hand to check every detail) seemed to frustrate Roger, as no sooner did he think he'd nailed a sequence than it changed.

The producers said he couldn't plug his book, *Bond On Bond*, as it was against BBC policy.

'Oh really?' he asked, before calling me to get a copy biked over to the studio. He kept it under his presenter's desk, and during the evening record, made a couple of very unsubtle plugs. Everyone loved it, and the BBC let his cheeky promotion slip through!

Though after a day rehearsing and filming, wrapping about 9.00 p.m., Roger was absolutely exhausted.

After eight weeks on the road, Roger and Kristina returned home to Switzerland, where soon after Professor Jichlinski called to say it was time Roger went back to the CHUV to have his kidneys checked again, as a matter of routine.

On 6 December, Roger reported for duty and the professor discovered the rhythm of his pacemaker was a little slow and so re-stimulated it, somehow or other, which put him back on a more even keel. Roger then had an MRI scan of his kidneys and whilst they were given the all-clear, there was some concern about another area on the scan.

It seemed there was some form of lesion on his liver, and in order to find out more the doctors wanted to take a biopsy the next day. Obviously he was concerned but they were so reassuring and said it was just a matter of routine. Following the biopsy, and although the word 'cancer' wasn't ever spoken aloud, Roger was told by Professor Dr Alban Denys at the CHUV that he'd need radiology followed by a combination of heavy chemicals fired at the lesion. Everything moved so quickly that he – and I – didn't have time to think about it. Kristina was absolutely amazing and an unwavering tower of both physical and psychological strength to Roger, even though she was terribly nervous, anxious and upset; but not once did she cry, complain or question why.

Again we only told only a handful of family and friends what was happening and reassured them that Roger felt all was going to be fine. Depending on how successful the initial treatment was, he potentially faced months of chemotherapy which was the only slightly daunting aspect of the whole affair – the thought of daily trips to the hospital would have placed more strain on him than anything else – ninety minutes each way.

Mercifully the first procedure was swift and the doctors felt satisfied they'd eradicated the tumour but cautioned the three-monthly check-up would be all-important. Only then would we really know how successful it had been.

We cleared his diary and were suitably evasive to all offers, invitations and thoughts of work; mind you, he was in no fit state to do anything as he spent most of the next few weeks in bed. Christmas at home was a more solemn occasion than I care to remember and while he remained confident he would make a full recovery, everyone around him was worried his poor old body had been put through so much in the last year ... but the old English actor wasn't going anywhere just yet. He slowly but surely bounced back to rude health. As each day passed, he felt increasingly confident that the long-term prognosis would be favourable, though in the few days leading up to his March check-up he did have a little wobble and seriously pondered his own mortality.

The drive to the CHUV was a fairly quiet one with no small talk or chit-chat. He told me he couldn't help but think about the wonderful good luck, happiness and fun life had afforded him ... and hoped there was still a bit left in the pot.

With huge sighs of relief and a tight squeeze of his hand from Kristina, the doctors gave him the thumbs up after the scan and said all was clear, with no further treatment required. His feeling of total elation, joy and gratitude when he phoned me was one I'll never forget.

One thing, however, was suggested to him by the doctors – that he gave up alcohol. He had in fact 'gone on the wagon' in the 1980s for a number of years and strangely the prospect of giving up his favourite tipples didn't bother him one iota. To quench his thirst he instead looked forward to a non-alcoholic beer or cranberry juice with fizzy water. He laughed about never waking up with a hangover too.

CHAPTER 17

ONE LUCKY BASTARD

Aside from the occasional Herberts who used to chase Roger – we've had them follow on motorbikes, in cars, on foot and even on trains – his genuine fans were a pretty nice bunch of people. Now and again one or two of them would call me via the Pinewood switchboard to ask if Roger had any upcoming film or TV appearances; though one lady, when she called, set alarm bells ringing.

'Politeness costs nothing,' Roger would say, and was always keen his fans were treated with respect and kindness, 'both of them,' he'd add.

On picking up the phone to this lady – I shall call her Pat – she asked me to put her through to Roger. Naturally I asked who she was and what it was about, and there was a pause; it sounded like she was crying, and she put the receiver down.

A few minutes later she called again, apologised for earlier, and said it was of a 'highly personal and sensitive nature' and she refused to tell me what it was. I thanked her for calling and said if she wouldn't divulge what she wanted to speak to him about I'd have to hang up – so I did.

I guess it must have been a week or so before she called again, and once more she asked to speak to Roger directly. Again I told her

I wasn't prepared to put her through to anyone unless I knew what it was about. There was a silence, followed by a little sob, and then a tearful revelation that Roger was her father.

Was she a prankster? No, I didn't think so – she actually sounded ill, and totally paranoid. I calmly asked why she thought Roger was her father, and she told me her mother was a cleaner at Elstree Studios in the 1960s and on her deathbed, a few weeks before, had confessed to Pat the secret she had supposedly been carrying with her for decades – the true identity of her real dad. Pat said she'd never known who he was, nor was he ever spoken about until then, and it had come to her as a huge shock.

This was the time of the dreaded *News of the World* stings, where the newspaper set up high-profile people in an attempt to see if they had any skeletons in the cupboard, and I did wonder if this was a potential set-up.

I asked Pat for her mother's full name, but she refused to give me anything other than a Christian name (similarly for herself – no surname was offered) as I thought I could at least try to substantiate if there was ever such an employee at Elstree.

Her reluctance, and reticence, made me want to end the call so I bid her good day.

I never mentioned anything to Roger about it and hoped it might be one of those things that just went away. But then Jean Diamond called, saying she'd had the girl on the phone wanting to speak to Roger, so I realised it wasn't just going to go away.

Sure enough, within a few days she called again – and always from a withheld number – to tell me she needed to speak to Roger as the 'deathbed confession' was eating away at her.

'What exactly is it you're looking for him to say?' I asked.

'I want him to take a DNA test,' she replied.

I simply hung up and resolved never to take a call from her again. She did keep calling the studio switchboard however, but they wouldn't put her through to me (the ladies on the switchboard felt she was 'very strange' too). However, one Sunday I had a call at home from Pinewood security – who fielded calls at the weekend – to say my sister had called in desperation as she'd supposedly lost my mobile number and needed to reach me urgently.

'But I don't have a sister,' I told them.

'We thought it seemed odd, and she seems strange, so wanted to check with you – we'll get rid of her.'

I probably didn't hear from her again for about a month. It wasn't Pat that phoned me but another lady, very professional sounding, who merely asked me to supply her with 'the legal counsel of Sir Roger Moore'.

I asked her to hold for a moment, whilst I googled her phone number (it wasn't withheld) and it came up as a firm of 'No win, no fee' solicitors in south London.

'May I ask what it is about?' I enquired.

'No. It's none of your business!' she snapped.

'Fair enough,' I replied, and put the phone down.

Within seconds she rang again.

'Did you just hang up on me?'

'Yes.'

'How dare you …' she snapped, so I hung up again.

On her third call she was a little more civil.

'I'm trying to ascertain who Sir Roger Moore's lawyer is, and you keep hanging up on me. Why?'

'Listen lady,' I started, 'you are not only rude and arrogant, you call me without any means of introduction, any niceties, and "demand" to know personal information about my high-profile employer. Tell me, if I phoned you and demanded information how would you react?

'Now, if you'd like to tell me what the nature of your enquiry is, I can then decide whether or not to put you in touch with Sir Roger's lawyer because I am acting in his best interests and my first priority is to ensure you're not some ambulance-chasing lawyer with a client professing to be his long lost daughter.'

There was a brief pause.

'Well, this is none of your business …' she began.

I interrupted her with, 'Then don't phone me again!' and hung up.

I now realised Pat had engaged a lawyer – albeit a second-rate one – so felt I should tell Roger about what had been happening.

Roger listened earnestly and said, 'Okay Gareth, would you take a letter …' I realised he was being very businesslike and serious, so without another word I picked up my pen and said, 'Go ahead.'

'Dear Sir/Madam,' he began, 'and you can look up the company name, can't you?

'I refer to your phone call to my office of today's date and the nature of your enquiry, which I feel I can satisfy here and now without the need for legal expense. Quite simply, you cannot get pregnant from a blow job.

Yours faithfully, Roger Moore.'

Well, I fell on the floor in fits of laughter.

'You can't say that!' I shrieked.

'Hmmmm. Okay, maybe not. But let's not do anything until something arrives in writing.'

All went quiet for a few months, and then Roger's lawyer at Harbottle and Lewis, Gerard, emailed – Pat's people had figured it out and had finally caught up with him.

'They're a small no win, no fee outfit,' I told Gerard.

'I shall write and, in no uncertain terms, inform them if they wish to pursue this course of action we will counter sue with a claim of slander and furthermore will be seeking substantial damages,' Gerard told me.

Harbottle and Lewis are also the queen's lawyers and one of the most highly regarded companies in the profession, so it may not come as a surprise to learn we heard nothing more from Pat's lawyers, or from her, ever again.

It would be ungentlemanly of me to suggest she needed psychiatric help, but sometimes you just have to stop being a gentleman.

On telling Roger's former co-star and friend Britt Ekland about this incident, she stopped cold.

'I wonder,' Britt said, and went on to describe how a few years earlier the stage door manager of a theatre in Swindon – where Britt was performing in pantomime – told her, 'Your daughter is here to see you.'

Her daughter, Victoria, was actually in Los Angeles, so Britt gingerly popped her head around the stage door to see who it was, and a rather wild-looking young woman called out, 'Mother!' as soon as she spotted Britt.

Britt naturally asked her who she was.

'I'm your daughter, and Roger Moore is my father,' came her reply.

'My dear young woman,' Britt answered, 'there are many things in life that are forgettable, but childbirth is certainly not one of them!'

With that, Britt turned on her heels and let the stage door manager dismiss the girl. Of course, I hadn't met 'Pat' so didn't know if she matched Britt's description, but it certainly made us think.

Our publishers, Michael O'Mara books, were delighted with the way *Bond On Bond* had been selling throughout the world, along with the paperback edition of *My Word is My Bond*.

'How about another volume of memoirs?' they asked.

'But we've covered everything in the two books, haven't we?' Roger asked me.

'Well, not quite. There were some stories cut – for reasons of space – and it's been five years since the first book was published,' I suggested.

'There's not enough to fill another book though,' Roger mused, 'so I'm really not sure.'

'How about a collection of stories and anecdotes, some first, some second-hand?' O'Mara said. 'As Roger has so many tales of his celebrity friends that he's been regaling audiences with on stage.'

'A sort of tales from Tinseltown?' Roger asked.

'Exactly,' came their reply.

He suggested I fly out to Switzerland for a week or two, 'and bring your recorder with you!' he added.

We again chatted and reminisced through Roger's life and all the people he'd met.

'I've been one lucky bastard,' he quipped. 'Hey, do you think they'd allow me to call the book that?'

It was certainly our working title, though whilst it stuck in the USA, the word back from UK booksellers was that they weren't quite sure priority space on shelves could be given to a book with a swear word in its title. 'It could prove tricky in promoting it on TV and radio too,' they cautioned.

Our lovely theatre producers also asked if we might have a chat. They felt the seven-date tour had gone remarkably and wondered if Roger would like to repeat it, maybe with a few more venues and a wider area. Roger thought it over for a few minutes before replying, 'Shall we see what theatres and dates they can come up with?' For him, that was as good as a 'yes'.

Leeds, Guildford, Watford, Reading, Salford, Birmingham, Glasgow, Edinburgh, Milton Keynes, Buxton and Wimbledon were all keen. Jeremy and Suzanna also suggested we add a little more production value with a screen behind, displaying images and maybe a bit of film footage – and that meant they could also have a couple of cameras on stage, trained on us, and project us onto the big screen for the benefit of the people sitting towards the back of the auditoriums who might miss every little naughty nuance or raised eyebrow Roger shared. Steve and Aron were the top technicians in charge and did a fantastic job of matching photos with our chat – which was in a rough order, but Roger often shot off at tangents. It also meant we could run a couple of clips, and during the interview offer up a text and tweet hashtag to #asksirroger, in order that we could take a mixture of tweets, texts and live questions. It was always handy to have a couple in hand as in between the microphone being passed to audience members, I could fire a couple of quick queries to Roger and everything moved without pause.

Though shortly before the tour kicked off, there was worrying news from Monaco.

In mid-September 2013, Roger complained of feeling terribly tired, incredibly thirsty and was losing weight quite drastically. Their regular doctor was away on holiday, and so another visited, drew some blood and said the results would be known shortly.

The dreaded word came up – 'hospital'.

Roger's blood sugar levels were dangerously high, and he was whisked straight in and onto an insulin drip where he was diagnosed as a 'type 2 diabetic'.

The next day he felt absolutely fine, though the doctors said they wanted to keep him in for a few days to monitor and work out the best course of medication. Having already given up alcohol, he happily smiled when they suggested he shouldn't drink, but then came the news of other things he'd need to cut back on: pasta, fatty meats, butter, sugar, cakes, ice cream. All his beloved treats.

He vowed to watch his diet closely, do as the doctor told him and probably live a healthier life for it. Thankfully he was diagnosed as 'fit to tour' and the show went on.

One of my tasks, between hotels and venues, was to find somewhere for lunch every day. Roger preferred a good old-fashioned pub lunch, and so armed with the *Good Pub* and *Michelin Guide* books, I plotted out routes that passed the best hostelries. Not only was my lunch on the line, my head was too – figuratively.

I always booked in Roger's name in the knowledge he'd be given a nice table and not – as Michael Winner used to complain in his restaurant review column – one next to the toilets or kitchen. Quite a few pubs obviously didn't expect the Roger I'd booked for it to be *the* 'Sir Roger Moore' by the pleasantly surprised looks on their faces. Roger always invited Stewart, our driver, and me to join him and Kristina for lunch. 'We travel together, we eat together,' he would say.

Rarely did anyone ever bother Roger, though on leaving he'd sometimes be asked for an autograph. Over the years, we managed to return to a few of the favoured pubs and restaurants and became quite friendly with the owners and managers; one of Roger's favourites was the Three Horseshoes in Breedon On The Hill, just off the M1 near East Midlands airport. Being in the centre of the country, we passed by once or twice a year and the owners Jenny, Stewart and Ian were people we always looked forward to seeing.

'We have some lovely cod in,' they'd say to Kristina, knowing it was her favourite dish, and Roger often enjoyed their fish and chips, 'with garden peas, not mushy,' he'd caution, 'and lots of tomato ketchup.'

'Bloody good food,' Roger would comment as we pulled out of the car park each time.

I think Roger enjoyed eating in pubs because they were usually relaxed, friendly and unpretentious – he could be himself, and just be 'ordinary' whilst eating the comfort food he'd grown up with, and the Three Horseshoes was just the sort of pub he could see himself behind the bar of, as publican, he would say.

Criss-crossing the country was fairly tiring, and Roger quite often took a snooze in the back of the people carrier, though he was never really quite asleep as we'd often discover – he used to joke that Stewart's satnav was last updated in 1975 and would say, 'He takes us on roads with tumbleweed blowing.' Quite often, if Stewart pulled onto a B-road, Roger would sarcastically call out, 'Found another shortcut Stew?' and then fall back to sleep. It became a running joke that Stewart would always look for a traffic jam to join, or farm track to cut through.

Roger treated Stewart as a friend, and Stewart was so very loyal, extremely helpful and would literally do anything for Roger.

Once or twice, pulling into pub car parks, Roger would tease him with, 'Thank you Stew, now go fuck off and find a BP garage, get yourself a sandwich and car wash and see you back here in an hour.'

Then he'd chuckle and say, 'Or you could join us?'

On quite a few occasions we were told, 'There's no charge,' when Roger asked for the bill. He was always genuinely touched and surprised, and always left a very generous tip behind.

Although travelling was tiring, it was always great fun and usually peppered with rude jokes and stories coming from the back seat.

After the bout of pneumonia and other health issues, Roger was visibly slower in 2013 in walking around and climbing stairs. He'd complain his knees were 'not what they used to be'.

On leaving for home at the end of the tour, I suggested he might benefit from a wheelchair at the airport – as his biggest grumble was the long walks through terminals.

'I don't know ...' he said. 'What if someone takes a photo?'

He was very conscious and proud of his image and didn't want to be seen as a feeble old man.

'If anyone asks, we'll just say you hurt your foot in an on-set trip and your ankle has swollen up,' I suggested.

Reluctantly Roger agreed to the wheelchair, and later phoned to say how much easier it was and how happy Kristina was that he didn't have to struggle. His 007 pride may have taken a slight bruising, but he realised accepting a little help wasn't a sign of weakness.

CHAPTER 18

SCOTCH EGG GATE

The year 2014 started off with a mix of offers – a Spanish TV chat show, recording a hologram to appear in a touring theatre show, fielding various press interviews and Roger being very vocal about animal welfare, foie gras and circus animals.

Having delivered the draft of his next book, and the title in the UK changed to *Last Man Standing*, reflecting the fact that Roger was the only one left from the line-up of Gregory Peck, David Niven, himself and Trevor Howard on the cover image, there was much to do in checking proofs, captioning photos and working with the PR team to come up with a promotion schedule.

The chance of another theatre tour, to tie in with publication, also came up.

Canterbury, Cardiff, Oxford, Brighton, Richmond, York, Torquay, Truro, Bromley, New Brighton, Northampton and Llandudno – over a month-long period – were all offered and though not an ideal geographical journey between each gig, it worked really well with a number of new pub stop-offs en route.

Travelling between Oxford and Brighton, I suggested a lunch at Pinewood – so I could pick up the mail, and so Roger could see his old friend J.J. Abrams, who was there directing *Star Wars: The Force Awakens*. It was all shrouded in the utmost secrecy and no one, but no one, was able to visit the set without special permission and signing non-disclosure agreements. Well, no one apart from Roger Moore!

Roger popped his head around the door of the production office to ask for J.J. Within seconds one of his producers greeted us, said J.J. was on the backlot shooting but there was a golf buggy at our disposal to head over. We were waved through security and straight onto the ice- and snow-covered set, where Harrison Ford was sitting with his leg strapped up (after an earlier accident) and J.J. with Kathleen Kennedy were standing next to the camera. J.J. came bounding over, hugged Roger and welcomed us all on set. They chatted for a few minutes, but seeing they were ready for a take, Roger made our excuses and we headed down to Brighton for our evening show. A couple of days later, Roger appeared on Graham Norton's radio show and innocently mentioned his *Star Wars* set visit and the snow – the internet was ablaze. This was the first precious nugget fans had of potential locations, and could it be ice planet Hoth?

'Have I put my foot in it?' Roger asked me later when he saw Twitter going crazy.

Speaking of Twitter, driving down to Truro we stopped at the Jack in the Green pub in Rockbeare. We enjoyed a good lunch and the landlord asked for a photograph as we were leaving, and within what seemed like minutes, that photo appeared on social media and the *Herald Express* newspaper picked up on it declaring, in their headline: '007 enjoys scotch egg on way to show in Devon.'

'I never had a scotch egg,' Roger said to me. 'Stewart stuffed his face with that. I had the ham hock terrine. Better tweet a correction!'

So we did just that, and minutes later the *Herald Express* broke the story:

'Breaking news: Sir Roger Moore shuns scotch egg for pork terrine.'

We fell about laughing at the ridiculousness of it all, but imagine our delight a couple of nights later when, back in our respective homes, we tuned into *Have I Got News for You* to find the exchange featured on the programme, with a lovely plug for the tour. Roger rang me immediately, 'Did you see …?'

'Yes!' I exclaimed. 'Great publicity.'

'I must write to thank them,' he said. 'Goodnight and see you tomorrow.'

Whilst in London, Roger agreed to film a guest appearance in *The Life of Rock with Brian Pern*. It was a programme that had appealed to Roger's sense of humour and realising he could film in his hotel room was the added bonus of it all.

We didn't travel on to the USA for promotion with this book, but Roger did participate in a lot of interviews via email, phone and over Skype.

In January 2015, Swisscom offered Roger a commercial. Filming in Zurich it was a fun gig, which paid quite well and was well made, well-lit and funny.

He then agreed to take part in an Australian documentary about George Lazenby – they headed to Crans-Montana in Switzerland and Roger spoke very graciously about Lazenby, saying he was glad the Aussie model turned actor had made just the one Bond film – as it left the path clear for Roger to take on the role. A few days later, Roger then filmed a sketch for *Comic Relief*, again in Switzerland, and then as a favour for writer/director Tom Kinninmont, filmed a cameo for his film *The Carer*.

This was all ahead of a planned trip to Paris in March to promote the new book, then to London for a recording of comedy quiz *Would I Lie to You* and a Jonathan Ross-hosted documentary on Pinewood

Studios. But that was all thrown into chaos when Roger phoned. 'My doctor says I've had a skin cancer come up on my leg, near my graft, and it needs to be removed. It's going to be a tricky one as there's no skin to pull over, and it'll need daily dressing changes. So I can't travel.'

I didn't want to say he had skin cancer, though Roger often made light of the little pieces of skin his dermatologist cut off over the years being kept in a jar, being almost enough to make a new version of him. I explained he had a leg injury and simply couldn't travel – they were all understandably upset and asked if we could reschedule for the following week, but this wasn't a wound that would heal in a week, so I had to be suitably evasive and apologetic.

It was a few weeks before Roger was fully mobile again, and we kept his diary suitably light.

He had agreed to a 2015 autumn tour, saying, 'This will probably be the last I should think.'

Theatres were so keen to book the tour that we were soon able to confirm Guildford, Cambridge, Blackpool, Nottingham, Liverpool, Bath, Harrogate (two shows), Cheltenham, Exeter (two shows) and Manchester. In between Liverpool and Bath, Roger had a few free days and we thought it best he stayed somewhere on the way to Bath rather than central London, as with Bath being a matinee performance, we'd need to get there by mid-morning. He settled on Bray and Oakley Court Hotel – home to the early Hammer horror films. He and Kristina loved the hotel, its setting next to the Thames, and raved about the food.

There, he was able to film for *Car SOS* which centred on the restoration of a Volvo P1800 as used in *The Saint*, and after filming, suggested that night we went to see the new Bond film, *Spectre*, the premiere of which was held in London when we were up in Liverpool. I booked the Everyman cinema in Gerrards Cross, and Stewart joined us too. We sat in the back row, and no one really twigged it was Roger until the manager welcomed everyone, ahead of the film starting, and hoped they'd all enjoy the film featuring 'the second-best James Bond' and waved to the back row. When the lights went up at the end of the film, and people started moving to the door, they began to talk in hushed tones, 'Roger Moore is here.' It must have been a totally surreal experience for the cinema-goers to realise they'd just watched a 007 adventure *with* a real-life 007 in the same room.

Liverpool had actually been one of the funniest tour venues – in terms of audience participation – 'Everyone is naturally funny,' Roger observed. One chap in particular should have had his own show, as he was hysterical. When it came to Q&As his hand was one of the first to shoot up.

'Sir Roger!' he exclaimed. 'It's a real pleasure to have you here. You're looking good. I mean, you've got it all – good looking, well dressed, debonair. As I stand here now looking at you, do you know what I'm thinking?'

'No, go on,' Roger laughed.

'You're a jammy bastard!'

The audience shrieked with laughter, and he continued, 'But that aside, I did have a serious question. Tell me, did you get to shag *all* the Bond girls?'

Roger burst into laughter, almost crying in fact. When he calmed down he said, 'But my wife is up there in the circle you know.'

'Go on, you can tell us,' our Scouser friend said.

Roger really loved the interaction and said, 'I think you should be up here, you're good,' to him.

'If they pay me the same as what you're getting, I'll gladly come up now!' he ended.

In Nottingham we had a slightly different audience interaction when we received a letter backstage from a young man, saying this evening was to be his and his girlfriend's first night out together since having a child a couple of years before, and as it was going to be such a special night wondered if Roger would help him do something – propose to his girlfriend.

'Do we know where they are sitting?' Roger asked.

'Yes,' our stage manager Mike said, 'it's all in the letter.'

'Right. Well ahead of the interval, we'll do that.'

Steve and Aron then arranged for a camera to zoom in and a light to shine on the couple so it could all be seen on the big screen.

'Just before you have a drink, we have a little announcement,' Roger said at the end of act one. 'There's a young couple here tonight in row N who are very much in love, and he has something to ask her' – he called out their names and the camera spun around to them. She screamed with excitement, as he fell to one knee and asked the question.

'What did she say?' Roger shouted out across the auditorium.

'She said yes!' he shouted back.

'Good. Come backstage and we'll have some champagne,' Roger added.

They did indeed come back and were both shaking with so much excitement that they could barely hold their champagne steady.

'It's massive enough that we're here in your dressing room, let alone him asking me to marry …' she said.

Roger introduced them to Kristina and said, 'If you're as happy being married as we are, then you have some very special times ahead.' He signed a photo and wished them both well with a kiss and a hug.

As we traversed the UK I noticed how Roger's politics seemed to change. In the north, the traditional Labour heartlands, he became left wing; whereas in the south he leaned very much to the right and the Tories. I thought I would pull him up on it during one of our shows, given the chance, as it was ammunition for a ribbing.

It was somewhere in the south, maybe Bromley, where the question of 'who do you vote for' arose.

'Oh, I'm very much a Conservative,' Roger answered.

'That never stopped you accepting a knighthood from Tony Blair's government though, did it?' I asked.

Roger feigned shock, and a slight deafness as the audience cheered.

'I must have been in the north that week,' Roger hit back with, as fast as anything, to equal cheers.

He'd often feign deafness if there was a question he didn't particularly like, and I'd quickly rephrase it into something I knew he could answer.

'Why did you hate Grace Jones?' being one such question.

'What was that?' he asked me, when pretending to tap his hearing aid.

'Did you enjoy working with Grace Jones?' I asked.

'Oh yes. Lovely chap,' Roger answered. 'Next question …?'

CHAPTER 19

FLOSSIE

Following the tour ending, Kristina was due to accept a 'Woman of the Year' award in Vienna. She was incredibly nervous and I think secretly wished she hadn't agreed to attend the ceremony. I travelled with them to the Austrian capital and Kristina's daughter, Christina Knudsen (known as 'Flossie') joined us too.

Flossie looked different – she had a yellow glow to her skin.

'Is everything okay?' Roger asked her.

She made light of it and said it was like a fake tan, and how amusing it all was.

'I really think you ought to see your doctor,' Roger cautioned. 'It's worth getting checked out.'

At the awards dinner, Flossie made the excuse of being tired to leave early and Roger thought he may have upset her as she'd requested being able to say a few words about her mother on stage, and Roger said it wasn't really appropriate. But Flossie was genuinely very tired and could barely keep her eyes open and in fact went straight to bed and fell fast asleep. She didn't want to join us for lunch the next day at the Sacher Hotel's restaurant, saying she didn't have much of an appetite, and that's when Roger became quite emphatic with her – 'You must phone your doctor as soon as you get home.'

A few days later, back in the UK, she did indeed see her doctor, who immediately sent her off for tests, fearing it was a liver-related problem – which her jaundiced appearance had suggested to Roger.

The news was far worse than anyone could have possibly anticipated: she had an aggressive and rare form of cancer, affecting the bile duct. It shocked us all – but none more so than Kristina. I cannot begin to comprehend how any mother would feel being told their child has a very grave and serious illness, and that if treatment was not started immediately there would be little time left.

Flossie was strong in spirit and in attitude and she vowed to fight the cancer with every ounce of strength and bravery she could muster.

The tumour sat at the base of the bile duct, leading into the pancreas, and had metastasised into the liver. Her oncologist's words were:

'You are living on the edge and if you tip over to the wrong side we are looking at a rapid decline, so we need to keep you on the right side of it.'

Roger and Kristina had been through so much with Roger's ill health in recent years, and just as it seemed all was well and they could all enjoy life, the 'bastard cancer', as Roger called it, changed everything and turned their lives upside down.

They flew to London to be with Flossie and stayed with her at her house in the country over the spring months, being a huge support. They took her to hospital and doctor appointments, helped look after the house and did the shopping. They, and two Danish friends, Kate and Carsten Hesselhoj, literally moved in with her and put their own lives on hold.

Roger had actually committed to another tour, at Flossie's behest as she wanted him to have something positive and constructive to think about. Needless to say, Roger felt incredibly guilty even thinking about work, as Flossie's illness cast a huge shadow of sadness over everything, but she urged him to go ahead and said she'd aim to be well enough to join us all on the road.

However, the cancer was aggressive and extremely ruthless. By the early summer, six months after being diagnosed, brave Flossie was admitted to hospital in London where Roger and Kristina joined her every day, to hold her hand and to try and keep her spirits up. Roger never gave up hope, and always remained optimistic, but the toll it was taking on Kristina was immense – seeing his wife in tears every day and not being able to help made him feel so very hopeless too.

'I really don't know what more I can do. If only I could take Flossie's place,' he said to me.

By mid-July it became a case of keeping Flossie comfortable and out of pain as the cancer had spread to her brain and she started drifting in and out of consciousness.

Roger became numb and was very quiet. Our conversations were short, and I cleared his diary of all business.

On 25 July, Roger phoned me in the late morning to say Flossie had succumbed to the disease.

'Her suffering is over, but I fear my darling's is going to be neverending now,' he told me.

In the weeks towards the end, Flossie was very practical and wanted to discuss her funeral – it was the most awful conversation Roger had ever had with anyone. Flossie wanted to be laid to rest wherever her mother planned to be buried and in turn Kristina said she wanted to rest wherever Roger chose to be.

'Denham,' was Roger's reply, 'near Pinewood.'

Roger shouldered all the immediate arrangements of the death certificate, calling the undertakers and so on, whilst trying to comfort Kristina.

He asked that I contact a local funeral company to make arrangements for Denham, and upon doing so I was informed the parish church only usually allowed residents of the village, or those with close family connections, to be buried there. I arranged for Roger to speak to the vicar and as it was Roger's wish it would be a family plot, there were no issues and plans went ahead for the internment.

It was a touching, very personal service and so very full of love.

Roger and Kristina returned to Flossie's home. After a week or so, Roger phoned me in a bit of a panic:

'How many days have I spent in the UK?'

As an overseas resident, he was only allowed ninety days each tax year; he rarely ever exceeded sixty days, but this particular year I worked out he'd spent eighty-eight. Whilst finance took second place to emotions and grief, Roger knew that if he exceeded his allowed days then he'd be subject to UK taxation for the rest of the year and 45 per cent of income was a big chunk to lose if not planned for.

I phoned his accountant and lawyer and they worked out he would be allowed to spend up to 120 days, because of exceptional circumstances, but anything beyond that would be impossible. We needed twenty-two days for his autumn tour and a few days for advance publicity interviews.

'Can you book us a flight tomorrow afternoon? I'll need to be gentle with Kristina, but we really do need to leave,' Roger said.

In the days and weeks after returning home, Roger said Kristina cried more tears than he thought humanly possible. He was so kind, so sensitive and so loving.

The upcoming tour actually provided Roger and Kristina with a glint of positivity in all their sadness, and although their thoughts rarely turned from Flossie, they both agreed it should go on as planned.

On 22 September, they flew into London for Roger to appear on *The One Show*, followed by a day of London press interviews, a trip to do similar in Manchester for a day, on to Dublin and then home again.

A few weeks later, on 12 November, they flew into Norwich to kick off the tour in the Theatre Royal and we then criss-crossed the country (and Ireland) from Newcastle to Wolverhampton, Belfast, Dublin, Southport, Aberdeen, Glasgow and London – it was all culminating with a show at the Royal Festival Hall.

In five years of touring we had pretty much been to all the number one theatres (a few of them twice) and our producers had already said it'd be tough to plan another tour without looking at some smaller venues.

'I'm getting too old, I'm nearly 90!' Roger lamented. 'I don't think I can do it again next year.'

'You said that last year,' I replied.

'I know. But we've played all the best haven't we?'

We didn't discuss it again but there was pretty much an unwritten understanding we'd be ending on the London date – and Roger was of the firm belief you should always bow out at the top.

The first few dates were great fun, and we discovered a few new pubs on our journey and in Belfast Kristina's son Hans joined them for a couple of days – I'm afraid Roger didn't share her love of him though!

On the night before our Belfast matinee, Roger took Kristina and Hans to a recommended seafood restaurant for dinner whilst Stewart and I enjoyed the hospitality of a pub across from our hotel – the Europa, which was said to be 'the most bombed hotel during the Troubles'. Incidentally, Roger was staying in the Hilary Clinton Suite, which was adjacent to the Titanic Suite.

'The *Titanic* only went down once,' he quipped as we walked by.

Anyhow, the next morning – around 10.00 a.m. – Roger called me and asked if I had a spare charger for an iPhone as he'd misplaced his. I said I'd pop up.

'I'm still in bed,' he cautioned. 'I've had terrible indigestion all damn night.'

He said the meal the night before was 'bloody delicious' but had cucumber in it, and cucumber always gave him heartburn.

'It's more of a dull ache under my ribcage now,' he told me. I suggested that could be gallstones and asked if he was well enough to do the show that afternoon.

'I'll be fine, I'll take some paracetamol. See you in an hour or so,' he said.

Sure enough, he was fine and we walked across to the theatre and had a great show with a terrific audience.

The next day we left for Dublin.

Doing his usual recce of the stage door drop-off area, after dropping Roger at his hotel, Stewart and I drove over to the theatre and said to the stage door keeper, 'We're here with Sir Roger Moore …'

'Mister Moore,' was his sharp reply. 'He's not a sir here.'

There were still some tensions between north and south of the border it, would seem.

A few days later, in the dressing room at Southport's theatre, Roger again complained of a dull ache in his ribcage – and unusually for him refused the pork pies I'd just bought from the local delicatessen. He took a paracetamol and off we went again onto the stage.

CHAPTER 20

THE FINAL SHOW

Heading up to Aberdeen, we stopped at a hotel in Perth which had been recommended. It was an old country house with a mile-long drive. Shortly before arriving it had started snowing, and was getting dark, which of course prompted Roger to rib Stewart about his satnav taking us on a scenic route. 'Will we arrive tonight do you think Stew?' he asked.

Up the long winding drive, we pulled up to the front door. The people carrier had a boot full of suitcases — we rarely travelled with less than eight — and I went in search of help, and a trolley.

'We don't have a porter,' the slightly harassed receptionist told me at the same time as a resident appeared asking him to 'open the bar'.

Just then, a fairly well-dressed man in his 60s appeared.

'Can I help?'

'Yes, I'm here with Sir Roger and Lady Moore. They're just getting their things together outside and I wondered if you had a luggage trolley?'

'No.'

'You don't?' I asked. 'Nothing at all?'

'When James finishes in the bar, he can help,' was the helpful suggestion.

'Okay, well can we get them straight to their rooms please?'

'They'll have to sign the register,' the man – who had since divulged he was the manager – stated.

'No, I'll do that for them. Can we get them straight in as Lady Moore is feeling the cold?'

'Just because they think they're celebrities doesn't mean they don't have to sign the register,' he continued.

'It doesn't matter who they are – they're cold, tired and want to get to their room. It's 6.00 p.m. and we've been on the road since breakfast time,' I pointed out.

With that he picked up a key, said, 'You can bring their luggage this way …' and walked off down the hallway.

We got them into the room, and then Stewart and I grabbed our bags out of the car.

'You two are upstairs,' the manager said, pointing at the staircase.

'Do we get shown to the room?' Stewart asked.

'I've just said, they're upstairs.'

It was quite apparent he wasn't going to help nor show us the way. 'Can we book for Sir Roger and Lady Moore to have dinner at 8.00 p.m.?' I asked.

'Aye.'

'And Stewart and I would like to eat in the bar please,' I added.

'Ah! The bar is closed on Wednesdays,' he said.

'But it's Thursday today,' Stewart replied.

'Even worse!' the manager snapped, and walked off.

Upstairs, the floorboards were rather creaky in the hallway and Stewart actually put his foot straight through one – obviously, not intentionally.

'I'm going to see Basil Fawlty,' he said, and marched off downstairs.

A few minutes later Roger phoned my mobile, asking why I wasn't answering my room phone.

'It hasn't rung,' I protested, before seeing the phone wire had actually been cut.

I marched downstairs to tell Mr Fawlty, who helpfully suggested he'd get it fixed the following week, and meanwhile moaned at Stewart asking him why he'd put his foot through the floor! He then said, under great duress, he'd move Stewart.

From a modest double room, Stewart was transferred to … the bridal suite!

Roger had actually told me Kristina was feeling a bit under the weather, possibly coming down with a cold, and would have room service but wanted us three boys to have a dinner. So we joined Roger in the restaurant for the most comical dinner of our lives. We were undoubtedly the youngest of the diners – who all seemed older than Roger – and the time-warp restaurant was like something from the 1920s with waiters wearing white gloves, being ever so pretentious – and failing miserably.

The menu boasted the speciality of the house was ice cream – fifty flavours, all made on site.

'Could I have one scoop of coffee please?' Roger asked. 'I'm diabetic so have to be careful and one scoop is just enough.'

I asked for salted caramel, and Stewart for mint choc chip.

'Sorry,' said the waiter on returning from the kitchen, 'we're out of coffee, don't have salted caramel and have just served the last mint choc chip.'

'Do you have a dark chocolate?' asked Roger.

'I'll go check, sir … ah, I'm afraid not.'

'How about a raspberry then?' Roger enquired.

'I'm afraid Chef said he hasn't made any of that,' came the reply.

'Well, what DO you have?' Roger asked through tears of laughter.

'I'll go and check,' the waiter responded.

A few minutes later he returned with exciting news …

'We have vanilla, strawberry or chef's surprise.'

Roger hated strawberries (along with coriander – they were the only two things he'd refuse to eat), so that was a no-no.

'Tell me,' he asked, 'what is chef's surprise?'

'I'll just go and ask ... it's vanilla AND strawberry mix,' he said proudly.

We shrieked with laughter.

'So of fifty flavours we can have anything we want so long as it's vanilla or strawberry?' asked Stewart.

'Yes, sir,' said the serious waiter.

Breakfast was no better. Roger and Kristina always had tea and toast in their room, so Stewart and I usually trotted into the hotel restaurant together and on this occasion a waitress intercepted us.

'You're with the big group – over there.' She pointed at a round table set for twelve.

'No, we're not,' I said.

'Yes you are – over there,' she insisted.

'No, it's just the two of us,' Stewart assured her, as we took a small table.

'But don't you want to sit with your friends?' she asked, before finally relenting.

I asked for some cereal, which was plonked down in front of me.

'Could I have a spoon please?' I requested.

She rolled her eyes, and said, 'That table over there is all laid up but you won't sit on it. I'll go find a spoon then I suppose.'

'Do you think they'll help with bags this morning?' Stewart asked.

We both laughed.

Though Basil Fawlty did ask if we'd enjoyed our stay and suggested we 'Do come again' as he hurriedly closed the front door behind us.

The Festival Hall was most certainly the biggest venue we'd played and it was pretty much sold out.

To riotous applause Roger walked on stage, and for the next hour and a half (there was no interval this time) had the audience in the palm of his hand. I had a little digital clock by our feet so I could keep an eye on the time, and as I watched the minutes tick down I realised this was probably going to be the last time we would ever share a stage together and became a little emotional – although thankfully held it together.

At the end of every show I always said, 'Ladies and Gentlemen … Sir Roger Moore …' and that always ensured a standing ovation for him. This time he didn't walk off stage; he waited for the applause to die down and as he gave me a customary handshake he publicly thanked me for 'making it all possible'.

It was the most emotional moment of my life – knowing I'd be walking off stage for the last time with him.

Backstage some friends and family joined us in champagne and pork pies, and celebrated another terrific tour. Roger looked at me across the room and smiled widely.

A couple of months earlier I'd been chatting with Michael O'Mara books about possibly updated and reissuing Roger's autobiography in time for his 90th birthday in October 2017. The paperback version was still selling well, and they said, 'How about another book instead – a new book?'

'But I think we've pretty much covered everything haven't we?' I questioned.

'Roger is about to turn 90. How about a book on age, on wisdom, on reaching that milestone? A book about what drives him, what annoys him, what delights him? It doesn't have to be a huge book, perhaps 25,000 words with some illustrations?' they replied.

I mentioned it to Roger.

'Do you reckon we could come up with something?' he asked.

'It could be a sort of book of grumbles, with positive stuff too, about what annoys you with getting older – you always say technology drives you mad for a start.'

'Okay. We'll put our thinking caps on. Shall we put some chapter headings together and work from there? I'll need to think of a way into it …' he concluded.

The next morning, he and Kristina flew home to Switzerland, and a day or two later he called me from his car.

'I'm going to see my doctor as that damn ache has returned to my ribcage,' he said.

'Do you think it's gallstones?' I asked.

'Could be, but I'll get it all checked.'

I didn't hear from him again that day, but the next day he called to say he had been X-rayed and they wanted to run some further tests. He sounded worried.

A day later he called me to say they'd found something — a lesion on the liver. Further tests were needed and he'd let me know, he said.

We had of course been here before, and Roger had successfully recovered so there was no reason for us to think otherwise this time. Though he then called with the worst news …

'I never expected this,' he started, 'I really didn't. They say it's very serious, and there's also something on one of my lungs — it's spread.'

I was shocked and totally numb.

'What's the prognosis?' I asked.

'If I don't start treatment — a few months.'

My throat went dry.

'And with treatment?' I asked — but he didn't really answer, just mumbled about tests and seeing how things went. Christmas was just a few days away, and he said, 'Try and have a good holiday, and don't worry. But keep this to yourself please.'

How could I not worry?

CHAPTER 21

THE LAST TRIP

Roger always phoned me on Christmas Day and as I usually spent it with my mum, he'd ask to speak to her to wish her season's greetings. He seemed positive and upbeat.

We exchanged a few emails, bouncing chapter ideas around, and then Roger was admitted to hospital in Lausanne (the CHUV) immediately after New Year for tests.

On 10 January he emailed me:

Just to let you know that all seems to be going well, here in the Chuv ... Tests yesterday went well, although it would appear that a stone has found its way out of the kidney and they are going to have a bash at putting a stent in to ease its passage ...

The liver biopsy went well, results will be forthcoming next week when they will also have the lung biopsy ready and the very efficient team of specialists will confer and decide what the next step will be ... No reason for gloom ... I am very happy that I am very good hands ... should be back in Crans on Thursday this week.

We spoke pretty much daily and four days later he sent another email update:

> I sit with two tubes dangling from my right kidney some urine and the other blood … on Monday they hope to be able to sit down with me and go through the results of the biopsies and discuss what the next move will be … first though the kidney problem has to be resolved …

The following week, he met with the doctors. There were a few engagements in his diary including one in Austria, which he emailed me about:

> I think it better if we let the Glocks know that the possibility of our being able to make the trip to Klagenfurt is negative. We had hoped that the original diagnosis hanging over my head would prove to not be true. Unfortunately it is and so we will have to accept that there is no way that we might be able make the trip no matter how much we looked forward to seeing you both once more.
> Sorry about this.

A combination of chemo and radiation therapy to shrink the tumours in his lung and liver was discussed which would be, hopefully, then followed by some surgery to remove as much of the cancer as possible.

We were all in a state of disbelief. Roger had always joked about being a hypochondriac, but he always took great care of himself and the slightest ache, pain, twitch or itch would see him consult with his GP and therefore they always caught everything in preliminary stages – this time however they hadn't. The first signs of discomfort – the dull ache under his ribcage in Belfast – was not the early warning sign we had anticipated; the cancer had spread through much of his liver and into part of his lungs.

Radiation therapy was to be the first course of treatment, and Roger knew he'd be in hospital for several weeks which worried him hugely – not for his own selfish reasons but because he knew it was a ninety-minute trip each way for Kristina to see him, and that she'd be alone in the house. Fortunately their Danish friends Kate and Carsten dropped everything and offered to move in with Kristina whilst Roger was in hospital, to keep her company and also to drive her to visit him.

His phone calls to me over the late January–mid-February period became a little more sporadic during his treatment, his voice became quite weak at times and he complained the radiation had 'burned' his throat, making it difficult to talk and to swallow food.

Several months before, I'd booked a short break to Cyprus in late February 2017 and when I was at Heathrow about to board, Roger phoned me.

'Kate and Carsten have to leave in just over a week, for family commitments, and I think I'll be coming home around then but I'm worried about Kristina – she won't be able to manage and needs some help. Would you come out for a week or two after you get back from Cyprus?' he asked.

'Well … yes … but wouldn't you prefer Deborah or one of the boys to be there?' I enquired.

'I'm asking YOU. We'd like you to come.'

'Of course I will. Absolutely. You don't need to ask twice. I get back on Thursday so how about I fly out on Saturday?'

'Thank you. I should warn you you'll have to cook as you know Kristina can't, and I won't be up to it,' he added.

'Honestly, it's not an issue. What do you fancy to eat?'

Roger laughed.

'Thank you, Gareth.'

I booked a flight for the following Saturday and left the return open.

I flew the familiar route to Geneva then took the two-hour train journey to Sierre, the thirty-minute funicular to Crans and then a taxi to the house. Whilst I was on the train, Roger phoned to check my arrival time and suggested he would order some Thai food from a local restaurant as he knew I'd be tired – as ever his first thoughts were for other people, and not himself.

When my taxi pulled up outside Chalet les Papillion – so named because of Kristina's love of butterflies – Roger opened the front door to greet me. I could see he was leaning on a crutch on his right arm. He looked pale, thin in the face and appeared quite frail.

'Lovely to see you mate. Not much of a welcome, me looking like shit, but it's good to see you,' he said, before adding, 'the food will be here in twenty minutes. You know where your room is, so go dump your stuff and we'll see you in the kitchen.'

Kristina was laying the kitchen dining table, and came bounding over to me as I walked through the chalet, and hugged me tightly. 'Thank you for coming,' she said, 'though I'm not sure how much work he'll be able to do.'

I obviously looked quizzically at her.

'You are here to work on the new book aren't you?' she asked.

Roger quickly changed the subject by asking if I'd like a drink. It was clear he didn't tell his wife I was there to look after them, as he probably didn't want her to feel she couldn't cope, so I played along and said I'd brought my recorder and hoped we could find time to chat. In truth, I really didn't know if we'd be able to progress with the new book – everything was up in the air.

The takeaway arrived, and we sat down to eat. Roger had a small medicine bottle next to him, and I noticed his voice was becoming more raspy. 'I find swallowing very painful, and need to take a little of this ...' he explained. It was liquid morphine.

'I've lost my appetite for food, and my taste buds have gone a bit strange,' he admitted, 'so I may not eat much though I promise I'll enjoy what I do eat.'

'We have friends visiting tomorrow,' Kristina added, 'and they're bringing food with them. They insisted. But on Monday, Janus is coming for the day and I'd like to cook lunch, so would you help?'

'I'll happily cook – just tell me what you'd like,' I replied.

She looked at Roger and he smiled widely. 'Roast chicken please,' he requested, 'with roast potatoes, Paxo stuffing, Bisto gravy and vegetables.'

'Oh, not fussy then,' I replied sarcastically.

It was then around 8.30 p.m. and Roger asked if I minded him and Kristina going upstairs to lie on the bed and watch TV. I could sense he was tired and said I'd tidy up and yes, they should go and rest.

Roger didn't get up the next day. He had planned to join us all for lunch, but Kristina said he felt too tired. I went upstairs to have a little chat with him, and to replace batteries in their cordless phone which had been playing up.

'Sorry to be so unsociable,' he said.

Kristina felt he'd taken a little too much morphine. 'It makes him very tired,' she said, 'but he needs to be careful how often he takes it. I know he's in pain but equally he wouldn't want to be lying in bed doped up all day.'

I felt really helpless, and thought about how I was going to tell our publisher that he was simply too ill to write the book, as it wasn't fair to let them think it was all going well.

The next morning, Monday, I made some toast and cereal and started writing a shopping list for lunch ingredients. Kristina came down to prepare their breakfast tray and said Roger seemed a little brighter.

Janus was due around 1.00 p.m., so I aimed to serve lunch shortly afterwards.

Soon after I returned from the supermarket, Roger appeared in the kitchen.

'Morning wanker, how are you? … So are we going to get on with this book then?'

My smile couldn't have been any wider – Roger was back!

We settled down in his TV room and I switched my recorder on.

'I like the chapter titles, but I've been thinking about the opening. I'd like to talk about smells and sounds – so many things trigger my memories and I'd like to reminisce about them.'

We chatted for an hour, and then I nipped off to pop the chicken and potatoes in the oven, before we chatted for another hour. Roger was clearly enjoying it and we covered so much ground.

Around 12.30 p.m. we wrapped and I disappeared into the kitchen.

I'm not saying I'm a brilliant cook – I'm functional – but there wasn't an ounce of flesh left on that bird. Roger devoured a whole chicken leg, a few potatoes and some vegetables – and then a bowl of Eton mess. It was all fairly easy to swallow, which was the key.

After lunch he and Janus chatted, and after Janus left I spent another hour with Roger chatting for the book.

His daughter Deborah phoned me to see how things were, and if he was eating. She was a little aghast that he'd had Eton mess, as he was diabetic, but I said, 'Deborah, whatever he can eat is good right now – I'll make sure he doesn't go too mad, but it's good to see him eat.'

The next day Roger requested cottage pie, and rice pudding. The day after it was steak and kidney, and semolina pudding, then on Thursday it was roast chicken again. They were clearly childhood comfort foods. Deborah was concerned he should eat more fish, but I said, 'Deborah, whatever Roger wants, Roger gets – it's not up for discussion.'

I know she meant well, but with his appetite being small it was important to tempt him with whatever he had a taste for.

He seemed to be getting stronger as the week progressed, and we chatted for hours on end for the book. By the Friday morning he even suggested we should all go out for lunch, to Michel Roux's restaurant '19'. He was a bit wobbly on his legs, but made sure he looked good, his hair was the way he liked to have it and he had a comfortable sweater on with his cord trousers.

We had soup to start, and cod as the main. Roger even managed a scoop of ice cream to follow.

He looked so much better and clearly enjoyed himself.

Kristina had been incredibly worried at the beginning of the week, and had urged to me to say all I wanted to say to Roger.

'This is bad,' she said, 'very bad. He might not beat this.'

She remained optimistic and hopeful, but a light had gone out in her eyes.

Their Danish friends were coming back on Saturday, and Roger suggested I might like to head home, as a few days later he was due back in hospital – having built his strength up – for more tests and possible surgery. I arranged to leave Saturday afternoon, as I knew having too many people around the house would worry and distract Kristina – she'd be concerned we were okay and would worry, and in turn Roger would worry about her worrying …!

I said I'd need to leave about 2.00 p.m. to catch the funicular.

'I'll drive you,' Roger said.

'No. I'll take a taxi,' I replied.

'I can't let you take a taxi …'

'Yes you can and I've booked it,' I countered.

There was some leftover chicken and cottage pie. Kristina said she'd like to have the chicken cold, with some bread, so I plated up the rest of the cottage pie with vegetables and left it in the microwave for her to warm up for Roger later on.

We were all feeling emotional. Roger kept thanking me for going, and Kristina thanked me for encouraging him to work and write the new book. 'It's given him purpose,' she said.

I certainly felt I was leaving Roger stronger and in a more positive mindset, though I also realised he was still very ill and this could be the last time we spent time together – but I put those thoughts out of my mind.

Roger was due back at the Chuv for treatment, but tragedy struck. He fell over in his bedroom and fractured his collar bone.

His arm was placed in a full cast which meant he couldn't have any MRI scans as planned, and treatment had to be paused. He phoned me and was very angry with himself, and said it was likely he'd have to go into hospital as being at home was going to be difficult. Fortunately, his friend Jorg suggested he could maybe transfer to a clinic in Crans itself – to build his strength, heal his collar bone and Kristina would only have a short drive to see him. Relief all round.

On 8 April he sent an email to friends:

For our update … we are still in Crans, K in the chalet and me at the clinic which is about ten minutes away … reason being that I had lost quite a bit of weight and muscle … so I have to get my shit together in order to face whatever they have in store for me at the hospital in Lausanne next month. It's a bit of a sod, but who said life was a bed of roses? Maybe we shall get to Monaco in a month or so … more of that as time passes.

Enjoy the spring!

He asked if I could courier him some Horlicks malted drink sachets and some Complan milkshakes. 'They're easy to swallow and I feel them giving me strength,' he told me. Every week or so I'd send a parcel over. I also sent some drawing materials as the publishers asked if Roger could add some sketches to the book – fortunately it was his left arm affected by the fall and he was right-handed, so could put pen to paper.

We spoke regularly over Skype, and as he received the chapters I'd typed up he ran through them with me making little additions, changes and corrections.

'It reads well,' he confirmed.

His calls became more sporadic after 12 April, as he was having physio sessions which exhausted him, and were all building towards early May – when he returned to the Chuv for follow-up tests.

Just ahead of his admission he gave me a few final notes to type up for the book.

'I think it's ready to submit,' he said.

Deborah flew out to Geneva, where she stayed with a friend, and made the daily trip to see her father at the Chuv in Lausanne. She took him lovely snacks, massaged his feet, combed his hair and generally pampered him whilst helping pass the long days. She phoned me regularly with updates, and just to chat – it was very difficult for her emotionally, but she wanted to remain strong for her father. Geoffrey visited him too and enthused Roger with plans for a documentary film he was making about 'How to win an Oscar', and Christian was there too.

On Saturday, 6 May, Deborah phoned me – but it wasn't her usual voice. It wasn't the usual Deborah.

'Dad has had the tests,' she said, 'and it's not good news.'

'In what way?' I asked.

'It's spread everywhere. He has maybe three weeks left to live.'

Her voice broke, she started crying and I shed tears too.

Whilst I knew the news might not be as we'd hoped, the shock hit me very hard. I literally couldn't speak. Yet I couldn't say anything to anyone. It was the most awful and stressful thing I've ever had to bottle up.

Later that day Christian phoned me and asked if we could talk the following Monday about 'the practicalities' of everything. I had to set emotions aside and help make the final arrangements for my friend.

CHAPTER 22

FAREWELL DEAR FRIEND

When the doctor came in to see Roger following those final tests, Deborah told me he said, 'Don't depress me. If it's bad news I don't want to know.'

The doctor then took Deborah aside and explained.

Roger never knew how long he had left, but instinctively knew it wasn't long.

Christian started liaising with the hospital to get Roger home. They were going to convert the ground-floor guest room into a 'hospital suite' for him, and wanted to make him as comfortable as possible.

There was also some business to be taken care of and Roger called for his financial and legal team to visit and ensure everything was in order. His first priority was Kristina – he wanted to ensure she could continue to enjoy life in their Swiss and Monaco homes – and that she'd never have to worry about money during her lifetime.

Christian said, 'When the time comes – and I hate even thinking about it – we will not be in any fit state to make an announcement or talk about it. So could you draft something for us? We can then release it to the media and hopefully they'll respect our need to be left alone?'

I drafted a statement, which was the exact same one released on 23 May.

I also spoke with a few key friends, including Roger's agent Jean Diamond, producer Barbara Broccoli, actors David Hedison and Maud Adams, and his former assistant Doris. I said it was now just a matter of weeks.

Within the next ten days, Roger's health deteriorated quickly and it simply wasn't possible to get him home, but he was transferred to Sion hospital about thirty minutes from the chalet. He was pretty much confined to his bed, with Kristina, Deborah and Christian at his side in shifts. They asked if I wanted to visit, and although I dearly wanted to see my friend, I didn't want to see him like that – I wanted to remember him as the Roger I knew.

Every time my phone rang, and I saw it was Deborah, I jumped out of my skin. But on 18 May she phoned to say he wanted to speak to me – it was a lovely surprise. His voice was weak, but oh so recognisable.

'Hello boyo, how are you?' he asked.

I scrambled to think of something to say, as I knew I couldn't ask how he was – I bloody well knew – so simply told him, 'It's so good to hear your voice.'

He then moaned in pain, and Deborah grabbed the phone.

'Don't worry darling, he's trying to get comfortable in bed and needs a pillow behind his back. I'll speak to you later.'

I relayed every update to Jean and Barbara, who told me they kept Roger in their thoughts every minute of the day.

On 19 May, Christian phoned. His voice was subdued and sombre.

'The doctors say he has a matter of hours left. His vital organs are beginning to close down.'

Again I felt numb. The day I knew would eventually have to come had arrived. I cried so very much.

But Roger wasn't quite ready to give up the life he so loved and relished, and he kept hanging on for four more days, and then soon after 2.30 p.m. on 23 May, Deborah phoned.

'He left us two minutes ago,' she said. 'He's gone. His suffering is over.'

A couple of minutes later, Kristina phoned me. She was totally lost for what to say. We all were.

A short while later Deborah phoned again and asked me to release the statement. I asked if the family had informed who they needed to, and she said they had. I duly posted the statement on Roger's official Twitter page and within minutes newsflashes were springing up on my phone, emails started pouring in and my mobile started ringing off the hook.

The outpouring of love, affection and admiration for this kind, generous and talented man was overwhelming. It still is now. Though it's hard to comprehend just how many lives he touched – as a friend, as a UNICEF ambassador, as an actor and as a hero – there were also complete strangers who he'd never met pouring their hearts out on social media; it seemed the whole world was mourning the loss of the Stockwell son of a policeman.

One of the messages was from my friend Nick Varley of Park Circus films – his company looked after the Bond back catalogue of films – and he asked if it would be okay with the family to declare the following Thursday 'World Roger Moore Day' and re-release two of his Bond films in cinemas around the globe, in aid of UNICEF.

I didn't need to check with the family, I knew the answer – a big YES.

The hours and days surrounding Roger's death seemed surreal. I found myself talking about him in the past tense, and yet felt he was every bit alive – his legacy was and is huge and the love immeasurable. It took a couple of days to respond to the emails and messages, and that's before I even looked at tweets and Facebook comments.

I spoke with Roger's legal and financial team who had spent some time with him towards the end, and they had discussed his final resting place: he had always said he wanted to be buried in Denham, but they in turn said it wouldn't be possible. Why? Quite simply, Roger was forced to go into tax exile in the late 1970s when income tax was up to 98 per cent, and since then he'd planned carefully to ensure what money he did earn would provide a comfortable 'pension' for him and his wife, meaning he was limited on how many days he could spend in the UK.

HMRC, however, don't even regard death as an excuse, and if it is proven that the intended resting place of an expat is on UK soil, then their estate is subject to UK tax.

Roger was a Monaco resident, where inheritance tax is zero, but by virtue of him being buried in the UK his estate would be taxed at 40 per cent.

'I really don't mind where I end up,' was his response. 'Don't let it be an issue.'

As such, Roger was cremated in Switzerland at a very private and very small ceremony and his ashes were taken to Monaco for the funeral at St Paul's Church where they were later interred in the Monte Carlo cemetery. When Deborah first called with details of the funeral and said it was to be on 10 June, my heart sank.

'That's my birthday,' I told her.

'Maybe it was meant to be? You know he loved you so much,' she replied.

On 9 June I was in the queue for boarding at Heathrow when I felt a tap on my shoulder. It was David Walliams. He was one of the small group of friends invited to the funeral – the family wanted to keep it intimate. Of course, many people, colleagues and friends, had requested details to attend but I told the family we should instead sug-

gest they attend a later 'celebration' event, when the family themselves wouldn't feel as raw.

Meanwhile Andrew M. Smith from Pinewood Studios had called me upon hearing the news of Roger's death to ask if there was anything they could do.

'We would like to name one of our stages after him,' Andrew said, 'if you and the family would approve?'

Roger had long regarded Pinewood as a home from home, and the thought of his name towering over the backlot in the years ahead would have ranked alongside the knighthood for him, I know.

I therefore suggested we might hold the celebration event at Pinewood, at the same time as inaugurating the stage … and suggested what would have been his 90th birthday weekend, 15 October 2017. The family agreed, and asked me to keep them updated with developments and if I needed them to do anything.

Roger's funeral was a small, tasteful and elegant affair. Prince Albert II of Monaco attended, and read passages – as did all the Moore children – and David Walliams read 'If' by Kipling.

Afterwards we gathered at the Hotel de Paris, to raise a glass and share memories of our friend.

It was the most emotional birthday I'd ever spent.

In the weeks and months leading to 15 October, I was fortunate to enrol some friends in aspects of the event: Julian Rachlin offered to play; Joan Collins, Michael Caine, Barbara Broccoli and Michael G. Wilson offered to share memories; and David Walliams too, on behalf of UNICEF. My friend Matthew Field spent countless hours helping assemble the most amazing selection of clips and I was fortunate to be able to secure the brilliant 'Q The Music' to play two of Roger's Bond themes, set against the Moore family scrapbook of photographs on screen. Dave Worrall designed a commemorative brochure, which Studio Canal paid for, and a group of good friends helped steward the event with me.

The most amazing part was Her Royal Highness The Countess of Wessex agreeing to attend and unveil the stage. It was called 'The Roger Moore Stage' rather than the 'Sir Roger ...' because on a film set Roger always believed everyone was equal. He was known as Rog or Roger to the crew, and in later filming assignments he'd always say 'it's just Roger' whenever anyone addressed him by his title – and so the stage naming reflected that informality he loved.

Eon Productions arranged for a Bollinger champagne reception, a most wonderful afternoon tea and brought along one of the white Lotus Esprit cars from *The Spy Who Loved Me*, whilst the owner of the *Persuaders!* Aston Martin DBS joined a white Volvo P1800 as seen in *The Saint* in positioning their vehicles on the sunny Pinewood lawns. It was the most perfect day, and with 300 guests in attendance ranging from international film stars, writers, composers, TV hosts, UNICEF staff and film producers to publicans, hoteliers, airport staff, doctors, tailors, dentists and even some fans. Every aspect of Roger's life was represented and celebrated during the joyous afternoon.

To witness the big burly stuntmen, who bravely doubled Roger as 007, crying summed it up for me. I held it together up until the last few minutes when the Moore children came on stage and said very nice things about me, whilst presenting me with a special engraved bowl.

'To Dad's favourite co-star, Love D, G & C.'

Everyone at Pinewood was fantastic. Eon went above and beyond. HRH remarked it was one of the most delightful afternoons, remembering 'a most wonderful human being'.

POSTSCRIPT

Life of course is now very different.

Driving to the office at Pinewood has lost some of its magic, though driving out – particularly in the dark evenings of winter – fills me with great pride when I see the Roger Moore Stage illuminated and his name up in lights. He'd have been so chuffed.

The final manuscript for his last book literally formed his last days of work. He was so keen it should be completed.

The title was changed from the proposed *Roger Moore: Getting On* to *À bientôt* – the final words in the book, which are French for 'see you soon'.

His films and books are his everlasting legacy, and when I spotted an old Pan paperback of his *Live And Let Die* diary on the office bookshelf I realised it had been out of print for forty-five years and started reading it – I read the whole book from cover to cover! It was too good a book to leave on a shelf gathering dust, and so I pitched the idea of republication to The History Press who immediately said, 'Yes! We'd love to bring it back.'

The 007 Diaries was published in 2018 in a limited edition hardback, followed up with a soft-cover version, which brought it to a whole new audience and very positive reviews. His friend and co-star, David Hedison, wrote a touching foreword.

Roger's five books take pride of place on many people's shelves, not least my own.

Books are one thing, but of course I miss him and our conversations like mad and I think about him every day: his humour, his panache and his ability to never take himself too seriously. Though equally he had a marvellous ability to turn an insult back on its server, such as when one of the *Daily Mail's* columnists took a swipe at his Bond films. Roger was a little irked and tweeted:

'Quentin Letts refers to my "silly renditions as 007". Fair enough, I thought, on my Monte Carlo balcony.'

Now, that is class.

I know I will never, ever, work with anyone like Roger again and I cherish the sixteen years I spent with him as being the very best of my life. I will remain fiercely loyal to his memory and his legacy as long as I live, and will never hear a bad word said against him because he *really* was a saint.